THE APOCALYPSE AND
THE THIRD MILLENNIUM

Isaiah
61

The Apocalypse and the Third Millennium

Today's Guide to the Book of Revelation

George T. Montague, S.M.

CHARIS

SERVANT PUBLICATIONS
ANN ARBOR, MICHIGAN

Expanded edition of book previously titled *The Apocalypse.*

Published by Servant Publications
P.O. Box 8617
Ann Arbor, Michigan 48107

98 99 00 01   10 9 8 7 6 5 4 3 2 1

Printed in the United States of America
ISBN 1-56955-106-5

Library of Congress Cataloging-in-Publication Data

Montague, George T.
   The Apocalypse and the third millennium: today's guide to the book of Revelation / George T. Montague.
      p. cm.
   Rev. ed. of: The Apocalypse. Ann Arbor, Mich. : Servant Publications, c1992.
   Includes bibliographical references.
   ISBN 1-56955-106-5 (alk paper)
   1. Bible. N.T. Revelation—Commentaries.   I. Montague, George T. Apocalypse.   II. Title.
   BS2825.3.M64   1998
   228'.07—dc21   98-28993
                                    CIP

Contents

ACKNOWLEDGMENT

I OWE A GREAT DEBT of thanks to my friends Suzy and Tom Crowley for their invaluable assistance in preparing the questions offered at the ends of the chapters.

Outline for the Book of Revelation

IN THE TABLE OF CONTENTS the book is divided into units that facilitate study. Following is a topical outline, which divides the book in keeping with the timeline on page 12.

Prologue (1:1-3)
Address and Greeting (1:4-9)
Inaugural Vision: The Son of Man (1:10-20)
What Is Happening Now (2:1-3:22)
The Immediate Future in Heaven: God and the Lamb (4:1-5:14)
The Immediate Future on Earth (6:1-19:21)
    A. The Seven Seals (6:1-7:17)
    B. The Seven Trumpets (8:1-11:19)
    C. The Unnumbered Visions (12:1-14:20)
    D. The Seven Plagues (15:1-16:21)
    E. The End of Babylon and the Nations (17:1-19:21)
The Longer Future: The Millennium (20:1-6)
The End (20:7-15)
The New Creation (21:1-22:5)
Epilogue (22:6-21)

The Seven Churches

ASIA MINOR

● PERGAMUM

● THYATIRA

● SMYRNA   ● SARDIS

● PHILADELPHIA

● EPHESUS

● LAODICEA

Patmos

Timeline

The Present and Future in the Book of Revelation

Now: The time perspective is that of John, the point at which he stands. Some of the churches have begun to experience persecution. It is a time of growth and purification, which is the theme of the letters, Chapters 1-3.

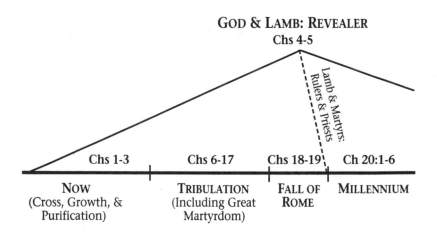

Great Tribulation: What is about to happen involves wars, bloodshed, and suffering from which the elect are not spared but are protected, Chapters 6-17. This ends with:

The Fall of Rome (Babylon): Chapters 18-19

The Millennium or 1000-Year Reign: 20:1-6

Timeline

The Present and Future in the Book of Revelation

Short Persecution and Final Battle: A new outbreak of short persecution on the international level is followed by cosmic war ending in the final battle, Gog and Magog (20:7-10).

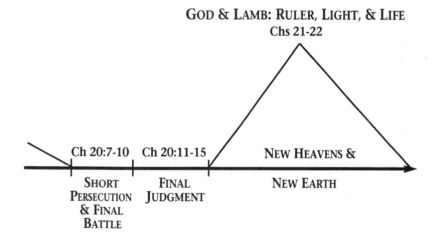

GOD & LAMB: RULER, LIGHT, & LIFE
Chs 21-22

Ch 20:7-10   Ch 20:11-15   NEW HEAVENS &

SHORT   FINAL   NEW EARTH
PERSECUTION JUDGMENT
& FINAL
BATTLE

Passing of the Present Age and the Final Judgment: (20:11-15).

New Heavens and New Earth: Chapters 21-22.

On the upper stage, in Chapters 4 and 5, God and the Lamb *reveal;* in Chapters 21-22 they *rule* in the new creation and the New Jerusalem.

The Apocalypse and the Third Millennium: Fever or Fervor?

THE WORLD IS IN CRISIS. The world's lungs, the Amazon rain forest, are drying into a tinderbox. If this forest catches fire, it could choke whole populations. Plankton, the very beginning of the world's food chain, is endangered. If global warming melts the polar ice significantly, it could raise the ocean levels twenty feet, and, as one newspaper put it, that would mean "Bye bye, Boston. Adios, Miami. New Orleans, adieu." The cold war between the superpowers ended only to see new forms of ethnic genocide emerge in Bosnia and Rwanda. And, as one authority warned, it's possible that some small but irresponsible country could have stockpiled enough biological weapons to wipe out civilization on earth. Family life is breaking down at an unprecedented rate, spawning more and more violence in our cities. The list could go on. One thing is certain: we are conscious as never before that our world is a global village and that its future will involve the whole human family in a way never dreamed of by generations past. (Ten percent of Los Angeles' smog comes from eastern Asia!) These scenarios make the future of our world a sobering prospect.

And a new millennium is upon us. Is the world coming to an end? Is Jesus coming soon? What response does the Word of God urge upon us? There are ostrich Christians who say that the problems are too big for them to deal with. Other Christians see them as *signs* of a message from God. And some of these maintain there is a connection between these events and the new millennium. And many of these say these events mark the countdown for the end of the world and the second coming of Christ.

MARKING TIME

Why do they make these connections? The earliest peoples on earth didn't. They thought of time in a static, or at least a cyclic, fashion. The seasons come, the seasons go, the world will always be the same. People were aware of good and evil, of course, but, judging from the Babylonian creation myth, where Marduk struggles with the goddess of chaos, most ancient peoples thought that the conflict of good and evil would be unending. In the sixth or seventh century B.C., Zoroaster taught that time is a process which would end ultimately in the triumph of the good god, Ahura Mazda, over Angra Mainyu, the god of evil and chaos. But elsewhere in the Near East there was a people already goal-oriented because of their covenant God. The Lord's word to Israel is that he is the God of history, moving the world and the people of God toward a goal that later Judaism called the kingdom or the reign of God. It is natural, then, that Bible-fed peoples and cultures strive to read God's plan in the ongoing events of the world.

One of those events for us is the arrival of the third millennium. There is something universally fascinating about the zero years, and even more so the thousand. Years marked by fifties or hundreds or thousands make people conscious of the flow of time, responding either with thanksgiving (as in jubilees) or with urgency. Of course the year 2000 is probably not precisely the two thousandth year after the birth of Christ. In the early centuries of

Christianity in the Roman empire, years were calculated from the founding of Rome. In A.D. 533 a monk, Denis the Little, proposed to reckon years from the birth of Christ. He chose the Roman year 754 and renamed it A.D. 1, not realizing that Herod the Great, who had to be living at the time of Jesus' birth, died in the Roman year 750. The mistake was discovered only centuries later, and corrected by Pope Gregory XIII in 1582. It is the Gregorian calendar that we follow today. A precise chronology, then, would put the birth of Jesus in 4 B.C. and his 2000th birthday in 1996! Like all calendar dates, the millennium is a human construct, without anything magical about it. In spite of that, it has not lost its universal fascination.

LOOKING TO THE MILLENNIUM IN THE APOCALYPSE

Among Christians, though, there is more than numerical fascination. There is the Apocalypse, with divine authority for believers. Its coded language and numbers provide unlimited speculation for those anxious to find allusions to today's world. This is especially true of the number 666 (one "locutionary" says that 666x3 = 1998, and this will begin an all-out attack by Freemasonry on the church). It is also true for the "thousand years" during which the author says the martyrs will reign with the glorious Christ (Rv 20:1-6, a text we examine in our commentary). That prophecy has fueled numerous interpretations, literal and allegorical. Does that millennium have anything to do with our third millennium?

The literal interpretation of Revelation 20:1-6 goes back quite early. For two centuries Christians suffered persecution and martyrdom under the boot of Roman emperors. They hoped that Christ would return soon and vindicate them. Irenaeus, Hippolytus, Justin, and Lactantius among others took the text literally as an earthly reign of a thousand years. But Saint Augustine, living in a period when Christianity was enjoying relative peace, took the thousand years as symbolic of the entire period of the church, and this became the prevailing view for centuries. Pope Gregory the Great, who lived in a time of great upheaval, believed that the end of the world was near, but he resisted any dating of it. Moreover, he built on Augustine's view by urging each Christian to become attentive to the Antichrist within one's own life, especially pride and hypocrisy, which make us precursors of the Antichrist or members of his body. In the tenth century a monk named Adso wrote an immensely popular book in which he said that the Antichrist is "anyone, layman, cleric or monk, who lives contrary to justice...and blasphemes what is good."

But some could not resist the attraction of literalism, both for the Antichrist and the millennium. The year 1000 raised the hopes of many that a new thousand-year reign would begin. In the eleventh century Tanchelm of Antwerp and in the twelfth, Joachim of Fiore and the Spiritual Franciscans saw a new age dawning. Unlike Augustine, Joachim and his followers identified specific characters as the literal meanings of the figures of the Apocalypse (e.g., Mohammed is the beast rising from the earth). After the Black Death, the fourteenth century witnessed a number of peasant uprisings based on millennial hopes. Konrad Schmid of Thuringia led the millennium-inspired Flagellant movement, which would carry over into the New World. The same hopes fired the Taborite wing of the Hussite reformers in the fifteenth century and the fiery preaching of the Dominican Savanarola, who proclaimed a seven-age theory of history that he found revealed in the Apocalypse. He saw the population of Florence, purified of vice, as the forerunner of the millennium. Similar hopes fueled the Peasants' War and the Anabaptist movement in the sixteenth century. In the seventeenth century, the Quakers in England held the literal sense of the millennium, as did the Pietists and Moravians in the Germany of the eighteenth century. So millennium fever is not a recent contagion.

In the nineteenth century a number of socialists (notably Karl Marx) used millennial categories in a secular way to fire hopes and actions for an ultimate perfect society. Today some Evangelicals like Hal Lindsey (who says his *Late Great Planet Earth* and its sequels have sold forty million copies) read in contemporary events a countdown to Armageddon and the end-time. Numerous Catholics take the multiplication of Marian apparitions as heralding a coming time of darkness after which God's purposes will be achieved.

The dawn of the third millennium adds fuel to the millennial fire. That fire can be experienced as fever—or fervor. Millennial fever is anxiety to *know* what is going to happen and when. Millennial fervor is longing for, praying for, and working for God's perfect rule here on earth.

THE GOSPELS AND THE FUTURE

What does the New Testament advise? Each of the synoptic Gospels has an "apocalyptic discourse," where the evangelists have compiled the sayings of Jesus about the future (Mk 13:1-37; Mt 24:1-25:46; Lk 21:5-38). In all three Gospels, Jesus' prediction of the fall of the temple leads the disciples to ask him for more instruction about the future. Jesus centers some of his advice around the temple, and the rest of it around the future in general until his final coming. He first tells his disciples what things are *not* signs of the end: wars, famines, earthquakes, and false messiahs. Don't read these as announcing his coming, he says, for "the end is not yet." He goes on to predict persecution and suffering, and, in the Gospel of Matthew, even internal dissensions in the community. When false messiahs and prophets appear, don't go looking for them either in the desert or in inner rooms, Jesus warns, for the coming of the Son of Man will be as public as lightning flashing across the sky (Mt 24:23-27). Even as the church suffers, it must first proclaim the gospel to all the nations, and only then will the end come (Mt 24:14; Luke calls this period "the time of the gentiles," Lk 21:24). So then there is an important agenda for the church even as she waits.

Are there no signs, then, that the final coming of the Son of Man is imminent? Jesus does say there will be cosmic signs: darkened sun and moon, stars falling from heaven. Are these signs to be interpreted literally? Perhaps. But in the Old Testament, precisely the same kind of imagery was used poetically to describe an "earth-shaking" historical event, like the death of Pharaoh (Ez 32:7-8) or the fall of Babylon (Is 13:10) or a devastating plague of locusts (Jl 2:10). In other words, Jesus is speaking in the stock language of biblical imagery, and he could be using cosmic poetic language to refer to events on the plane of human history.

If that is so, it helps us to understand the puzzling example of the fig tree: when you see its buds you know summer in near, so when you see these things taking place, "know that he is near, at the very gates" (Mt 24:33; Mk 13:29) or "know that the kingdom of God is near" (Lk 21:31). And then Jesus goes on to say, "Truly I tell you, this generation will not pass away until all these things have taken place" (Mt 24:34; Mk 13:30; Lk 21:32). Does "this generation" refer to those listening to Jesus during his public ministry, or does it refer to the whole human generation until the end of time? And is it possible to say that even after two thousand years, the glorious Christ is near, even at the gates?

THE END IS NOW

Properly understood, the answer is "yes." It is helpful here to distinguish between *chronological* time and what has been called *kairos* time. *Chronos* and *kairos* are two Greek words for time. *Chronos*, or chronological time, is time as measured by the ticking of a clock or a surveillance camera in a convenience store. Neither the clock nor the surveillance camera makes any judgment on the relative importance of what passes in front of it. *Kairos* time, on the other hand, means time in the sense in which we say, "I had the time of my life at the party," or, "Now is the time to act." *Kairos* means an important or significant moment within chronological time. If you were to write your autobiography following chronological time, you would have to describe every successive act you ever did, and it would take you the rest of your life to do it and you would produce a very boring book. You could write a very interesting story, though, if you selected important turning points in your life, if, in other words, you wrote about *kairos* times. Now, within *kairos* time there is what we could call *rehearsal* time. For example, something happens that makes you experience the end of your life in the middle—a near-death experience which leads you to reevaluate your life. It is in that sense that historical events, wars, tragedies, earthquakes, floods, and other such phenomena can become the end anticipated in the middle. Thus Jesus and the biblical authors can see that cataclysmic event of the destruction of the temple as a rehearsal for the end of the world. The end of the one portrays and anticipates the end of the other. Whether it happens immediately in chronological time is not particularly relevant: in the immediate event you have met the final event.

This is the sense in which the Gospels invite us to read the upheavals of the present world order as forerunners of the final consummation of all things. That reading does not give us a precise chronological date (nowhere is that prophesied in the New Testament), but it does mean that the end and the coming of Jesus is *near*. And Jesus' advice, and that of Paul, is to live each moment in the light of the imminent coming of Christ. Thus the command: "I say to all, 'Watch!'" (Mk 13:37).

WATCHING

And what does it mean to *watch*? It doesn't mean standing with our eyes fixed on the sky. The angel upbraided the first disciples for doing that after Jesus had ascended (Acts 1:11). It doesn't mean speculating about the date of the Lord's coming: "It is not for you to know the times and dates that the Father has set by his own authority" (Acts 1:7). It means indeed praying, "Thy kingdom come, thy will be done *on earth* as it is in heaven." But it also means action. It means carrying the gospel in the power of the Holy Spirit to the ends of the earth (Acts 1:8). It means making good use of the present. Read what follows Jesus' apocalyptic discourse in Matthew 25. These are all parables aimed at inspiring Christians to be active in good works. The five faithful bridesmaids had the oil of good works in their lamps, whereas the unfaithful ones did not (Mt 25:1-13; see 5:14-16). The men who put their talents to work entered into the joy of their Lord, while the one who did nothing was cast out (Mt 25:14-30). And in the climactic parable of the last judgment, the sheep and goats are separated on the basis of their active or inactive charity (Mt 25:31-46). Those condemned in the final judgment are condemned for their acts of *omission!*

THE APOCALYPSE AND THE THIRD MILLENNIUM

The Apocalypse echoes Jesus' synoptic discourse. It is, of course, more extensive, but there are many parallels: the temple is no more; there are cosmic and historical signs aplenty (more specific and graphic than in the Gospels) and persecution and martyrdom; Jesus, the glorious Son of Man, is coming soon; and John makes the gospel exhortation to "watch, for you know not the hour" concrete by evaluating the spiritual status of the seven churches. The evaluations are of two kinds: on the one hand, praise and thanksgiving for the good things God's grace has achieved in the communities and, on the other, an indictment of particular sins with a call to repent.

The third millennium is a providential occasion to hear the Lord addressing our churches with a similar evaluation. The church and the world have basked in the effects of Christ's love and grace for two thousand years. Pope John Paul II called the church to a three-year preparation for the two thousandth birthday of Christ. What a great opportunity to give thanks! Reading the Apocalypse in the light of the millennium also reminds us that Jesus is not just one outstanding leader among others. He is the Lord of history. It reminds us of the end of all things, the consummation of all in God. And the military images that appear in the Apocalypse remind us that we must battle against evil in our world and we must do it with a united front. John's book leaves little room for grey areas. It resolves the dynamics of this world into their ultimate categories, good and evil, black and white. It sounds a healthy wake-up call for us who live in a grey world and so easily adjust to it. John calls us to purity of heart, purity of vision, decisiveness, and courage. He reminds us that our real struggle is not against flesh and blood but against the principalities and the powers, the evil spirits who rule the dark world (Eph 6:12). But the

Lamb has already conquered, and our warfare is a mop-up operation. Nowhere in the Apocalypse, however, are we told to take up arms in a literal, military sense. Our call is to spiritual warfare, not the demonizing of other people and the stockpiling of weapons as did the tragic Branch Davidians of Waco.

Reading the Apocalypse in the light of the millennium also tells us that our two thousand years have not been without sin, individual and collective. Besides the many failings of Christians in the past, there is what we have *not* done, our sins of omission. While we rejoice that the faith has spread throughout the world, we are also reminded that more than half the world is not Christian. What have we done to evangelize? Have we hidden the Light of the world under a bushel? Have we conformed so much to the culture that we are hardly distinguishable from it? Are we more chameleon than Christian? How do the parables of the bridesmaids, the talents, and the final judgment challenge us? Do we find ourselves in the letters of the Apocalypse? Does the arrival of the third millennium raise our fever to know the future or our fervor to use the present?

"BE NOT AFRAID!"

But even when we do our best to live in readiness (and who of us always does our best?), we are not in total control of the world. But Someone is. And that is why the Apocalypse is a book of hope. Even John's descriptions of troubles to come fit into his much larger aim, which is not to frighten Christians but to reassure them. When John describes apocalyptic horrors it's as if he is saying, "Imagine the worst possible scenario—you will survive and triumph because God and Christ will win in the end." "In the world you will have trouble, but take courage, I have conquered the world" (Jn 16:33). The Apocalypse is a call to hope. It was on this note that Pope John Paul II concluded his *Crossing the Threshold of Hope:*

> *At the end of the second millennium, we need, perhaps more than ever,* the words of the Risen Christ: "Be not afraid!" Man who, even after the fall of Communism, has not stopped being afraid and who truly has many reasons for feeling this way, needs to hear these words. Nations need to hear them, especially those nations that have been reborn after the fall of the Communist empire, as well as those that witnessed this event from the outside. Peoples and nations of the entire world need to hear these words. *Their conscience needs to grow in the certainty that Someone exists who holds in His hands the destiny of this passing world; Someone who holds the keys to death and the netherworld* (cf. Rev. 1:18); *Someone who is the Alpha and the Omega of human history* (cf. Rev. 22:13)—be it the individual or collective history. And this Someone is Love (cf. 1 Jn 4:8, 16)—Love that became man, Love crucified and risen, Love unceasingly present among men. It is Eucharistic Love. It is the infinite source of communion. He alone can give the ultimate assurance when He says, "Be not afraid!"

May your reading of the Apocalypse enable you to enter the third millennium bearing the victorious banner of the King of Kings and Lord of Lords! May the millennial fire burn in you not as fever but as fervor—active fervor—for the coming of his kingdom!

Now, as you read the Book of Revelation at the turn of the millennium, keep in mind the following:

• Look first for the original meaning of the text for John and his readers.

- Then look for the counterpart in today's world. In so doing, see the Apocalypse not as a book to decipher but rather as a call to live our Christian witness and to remake the world in God's plan. Remember that goodness is incarnate in Jesus Christ. Evil has never become incarnate, although people and institutions can play demonic roles. We may reflect on who or what is fulfilling these roles today, for the Apocalypse is replayed in every generation. But with John, focus on the victory of the Lamb.

- The Apocalypse is a book for the persecuted church. More of our Christian brothers and sisters have been martyred in the twentieth century than in any other. At the turn of the millennium it's time for the rest of us to hear God saying: "Remember those who are in prison, as though you were in prison with them; those who are being tortured, as though you yourselves were being tortured" (Heb 13:3).

- Time is precious. Allow yourself to feel the urgency of conversion. As the Apocalypse urges this, so does the millennium.

Introduction

THE BOOK OF REVELATION or *The Apocalypse,* from the Greek word meaning revelation, is one of the most beautiful and most complex in the New Testament.

Most beautiful: Where else in the Scripture do we find such a wealth of biblical and poetic titles applied to Christ: Key of David, Morning Star, Son of Man, King of Kings, Lord of Lords, Alpha and Omega, the One Who Lives, the Lion of Judah, the One Who Holds the Seven Stars, the Holy One, the True, the Amen, and the Faithful Witness? Above all, in no other book of the Bible is the image of the Lamb exploited for all its richness to give us an understanding of who Jesus is—the Lamb slain yet standing. He is the one sacrificed for our sins, yet risen and living and now sharing the throne of God.

Where else is there such a profound vision of God's people as the New Jerusalem, the City of God, watered by the river of life flowing from the throne of God and the Lamb? Where else in the New Testament is there such a rich series of invitations to union with Christ, the Bridegroom? He is the One who stands at the door and knocks, promising to sup with his faithful followers, to give them the crown of life, to let them see him face to face with no more night or tears, and not even temple or lamp to obscure the divine intimacy. Revelation is also the most liturgical of all the New

Testament books—hymns repeatedly interrupt the narrative, often as part of an elaborate heavenly liturgy.

Most complex: Certainly no book has given rise to so many conflicting interpretations. Is it a coded message for our times? Is the Beast a prophecy about Russia, or Saddam Hussein, or the secular state, or even apostate Christianity? Can we detect from the book's bizarre imagery a countdown for the destruction of the world and the second coming of Christ? What are we to make of the "first" and "second" resurrections and the thousand-year reign portrayed in Chapter 20? How are we to interpret the vision of the seven trumpets with its interruptions and new beginnings? And the seven bowls? Often it seems everything comes to an end, only to begin again.

We in the twentieth century are not the first to have mixed feelings about this beautiful and complex book. It took a long time for Revelation to gain universal acceptance in the church and finally to be admitted into the canon of inspired writings. Even Jerome, the great early church father who translated the Bible into Latin, had his hesitations about it. Nevertheless, it was eventually accepted by all orthodox Christians as divinely inspired. This means that even today the church listens to it as God's Word having a *now* meaning.

To get at that *now* meaning, however, it is not sufficient for us to read into the text whatever interpretation may strike our fancy. Nor should we automatically project the benevolent or destructive powers we experience today upon this ancient text. This method uses the visions of Revelation like a celestial Rorschach test which tells us more about the interpreter than about the book itself. The first step in accurate and balanced interpretation is to try to discover what the human author meant for the audience for which he wrote. While the book continues to speak powerfully to succeeding generations, its author had a particular audience and a particular situation in mind. To discover this, in the case of

Revelation, may take more than the usual discipline and patience.

There are several questions that will surface in your study: What are we to make of the wrath of God? If this book is for the martyrs, how can it be of help to the rest of us? Is Revelation about heaven or earth? Is the material universe to be destroyed? If so, how does this do credit to God the Creator? These are questions which *you* (and the group you might share with) will need to grapple with as you move through the text. To help guide you, I have included sections at the end of chapters for prayer, reflection, and group discussion. These sections could be used as resources for a parish Bible study on the Book of Revelation, or simply for personal or family prayer, reflection, and study.

WHAT KIND OF BOOK?

When taking a book from a library shelf, it is helpful to know at the beginning whether it claims to be a biography, a novel, a play, a historical study, a philosophy, or poetry. In the Bible, which is in itself a library, how do we classify this book? *Apokalypsis* ("Revelation") is its first word. From this title some scholars have assumed that the book belongs to a type of Jewish literature that became increasingly popular around the time of Christ, called *apocalyptic literature*.

Indeed, many of this literature's features are to be found here:

1. a fascination with symbols, with symbolic colors and numbers (seven, three, and twelve and their multiples);

2. the themes of heavenly battle and cosmic catastrophe;

3. the description of present political powers in terms of past ones (Rome as Babylon, the people of God as Jerusalem);

4. the life-and-death struggle of the kingdom of God and the kingdom of the world.

There are differences too. Jewish apocalyptic works usually claimed to have been written in some past age as a prediction of the present. They were usually attributed to some well-known biblical character of the past, such as Abraham or Moses or Enoch. Neither the artificial setting of the past nor pseudonymity is found in Revelation. Its author writes for the contemporary church which is struggling for survival in the midst of a hostile world system. The church is enduring persecution or on the verge of it.

The author also identifies himself by name as John, one of the persecuted. Unlike the Jewish apocalyptists who wrote esoteric works, John receives the command not to seal the book (22:10); the book is to be read publicly in the liturgy (1:3). Other apocalyptic works often speculated on the distant past of creation and looked forward to the coming of God's kingdom as deliverance from, and reward for, the present suffering. John's apocalypse speculates very little about the past—except for one event, the death and resurrection of Jesus. And while it does look to the future, that future is not a sudden, miraculous rescue from suffering, as some advocates of the "rapture" theory today would have it. The persecutions which the church is presently experiencing are going to get worse. The church will have to pass through its own passion in imitation of, and in union with, the first martyr—Jesus.

But the victory is already won in him. That is why the great motive of hope is not future but past. The Messiah has already come! For all its frightening scenarios, Revelation is a book of incredible hope—a symphony of victory songs that can be sung, even as the church passes through the sea of its own blood. So while the book has some traits of apocalyptic writings, we are better off to accept its own repeated claim to be *prophecy* (1:3; 22:7,10,18-19). Prophecy and prophets were commonplace in the first-century church. Here we have an example of what one type of prophecy looked like.

REVELATION'S AUTHOR

An impressive number of church fathers in the first few centuries (Justin, Irenaeus, Hippolytus, Tertullian, and Origen) held that the fourth Gospel and Revelation had the same author: John the apostle. Indeed, internal evidence in Revelation, especially its rich images, shows an acquaintance with the tradition found in this Gospel. However, the author of Revelation calls himself a prophet, not an apostle. The apostles, described as the foundations of the city wall (21:14), seem to belong to the past. There is enormous difference in the Greek style of these two books. The Greek of the Gospel is exalted and beautiful; that of Revelation, inaccurate and sometimes crude.

Most scholars today think that neither the Gospel of John in its present form nor Revelation was written by the apostle John, although the apostle may stand behind the tradition as its "authority." According to Papias in the early second century, there was another John in Ephesus called John the Presbyter. Scholars around the turn of the century thought he was the writer. But Revelation's author never calls himself presbyter. Recent scholarship has rejected this solution. J.M. Ford (Anchor Bible commentary) proposed John the Baptist for the source of most of Revelation (a later author having "Christianized" it). Since most modern scholars consider the unity of the book to be unquestionably established (rather than being a compilation of sources), this hypothesis has had little success.

In any case, we can be certain that John was a prophet. Either he was one of the itinerant prophets common in the church in the latter part of the first century or a "settled" prophet (possibly a leading prophet or head of a circle of prophets). He does not appeal to any office other than his prophetic one. He understood his authority, like that of other New Testament prophets, as coming directly from God through revelation. He was probably a Jew by birth, for his Greek is very imperfect and "Jewish." His knowledge of the Hebrew Bible is so profound that he alludes to it constantly, freely adjusting its imagery to a new Christian register. He was acquainted with other Christian revelatory literature, or at least the tradition behind these works, for there are important similarities of his work with the Sibylline Oracles, some of which were written a few years before Revelation.

TIME FRAME

Irenaeus (*Adv. Haer.* 5.30.3) says that the Book of Revelation began to circulate at the end of the reign of Emperor Domitian (A.D. 81–96). Though this would allow for the book to have been written earlier, most authorities accept the witness of Irenaeus and place its composition around A.D. 95. The reasoning is as follows. Revelation shows throughout that it was written during a time of persecution, with the prospect that the persecution will soon become more intense. The basic issue was the demand being put upon the Christians to worship the Roman emperor. Caligula (A.D. 37–41) was the first to demand such worship.

But Revelation could hardly have been written that early—not only because it shows a theological development characteristic of the later decades, but because in 13:18 there is an almost certain allusion to Nero (A.D. 54-68). Was it written then under Nero? There are indications of an even later date. For example, Revelation uses the term "Babylon" to describe Rome as the second destroyer of Jerusalem. This is a usage which appears in Jewish literature only after the fall of that city in A.D. 70. The convergence of these elements with others appears to confirm that the book was written around A.D. 95 during Domitian's reign.

Apparently Domitian himself did not vigorously promote his worship. But there is evidence that the local authorities—the priests in charge of the pagan temples in Asia Minor—did so, perhaps with the idea of ingratiating themselves with Rome. The manner and intensity of its promotion could therefore have varied considerably from one city to another, as the letters to the churches seem to indicate (Chapters 2-3).

Some of the churches, especially the poorer ones, have suffered more, while a wealthier one like Laodicea was hardly suffering at all—in fact it needs to be awakened to the gravity of the situation. This suggests that, as often happens, the wealthy were able to ingratiate themselves with the local authorities more readily. Perhaps they even participated in the pagan banquets of the guilds to which they belonged and thus, directly or indirectly, shared in pagan rites.

John has a clear message. There is to be no compromising with pagan worship of any kind, especially not the worship of the emperor. He also expects the persecution to get worse. He writes to encourage the Christians to remain faithful even unto death. The alternative is eternal punishment. The reward of fidelity is twofold: eternal life and (as we shall see in this book) an impact on the earthly progress of history toward the kingdom of God.

LITERARY TECHNIQUES

If we want to understand the message of Revelation correctly, we must first learn to appreciate the methods and techniques John uses. He presents his work as *prophecy*. It is a revelation directly from God. Yet the literary forms in which this revelation is presented are varied. There is *vision, voice,* and *letter.* The author uses the *Old Testament,* but he never cites it formally. He uses Scripture passages like bits of glass that a glassblower melts to form something new. He does not quote Scripture to prove his point. Like the ancient prophets themselves, he speaks with his own authority, even when he uses the language and expressions of those who prophesied before him. He sometimes fuses Old Testament prophecies to show that their fulfillment is yet to come—as he does in 1:7 by combining Daniel 7:13 and Zechariah 12:10-14.

Most important is his use of *symbols from the past* to describe a present or future person or event: Balaam and Jezebel are code names for their contemporary counterparts. Babylon is a code name for Rome. The allusion to Nero (in 13:18) is probably a code name for the presently reigning Domitian. *Colors* are also symbolic: white for victory and purity, black for death, red for war, and green for plague. *Numbers* have a special fascination for John. There are four sets of sevens which divide the book: a set of seven letters and three sets of seven visions. "Thousand" stands for a large number, three-and-a-half for a short time, the half of seven. And so on.

Hymns or songs play an important interpretive role in Revelation, as they do in Greek tragedies. These are generally sung in heaven in response to, or in preparation for, some action on earth. There is thus what could be called the *two-tiered stage* or *split-screen* technique. The author uses this to describe what is going on in heaven, while something else is happening on earth. His literary camera often switches back and forth to show the interrelation of the two actions. The *plot* follows a timeline (see the illustration on p. 12). But the series of seven visions of the great tribulation are *interlocked* in such a way that the last of one series opens up the next series. These series do not follow an exact timeline but are rather new ways of presenting the same mystery of sacred history.

WHAT ON EARTH IS REVELATION TALKING ABOUT?

Since Revelation is concerned with the future more than any other New Testament book, it is understandable that theories have abounded as to what events have fulfilled or will fulfill the prophecies contained there. There is little dispute as to the meaning of John's moral exhortations. But what historical events is he portraying? There are three major ways of interpreting these:

1. Revelation is talking about events and persons of OUR time. In this interpretation, the book is a coded message in which the persons and events of our day, and what is about to happen soon, can be identified. This literalist interpretation is among the oldest. One of the Montanists in the second century maintained that the heavenly Jerusalem would descend near the village of Pepuza, in the region of Phrygia, not far from the seven cities addressed in Revelation. In our times the person numbered 666 was identified as Mussolini or Hitler or Stalin. The Beast is Russia, or products from the People's Republic of China are marked with 666, the number of the Beast. Some fundamentalist churches even today say that the whore of Babylon is the Roman Catholic Church.

The problem with this method of interpretation is that it is wholly subjective and arbitrary. With a little ingenuity, I can make the images of Revelation fit anybody I choose. Usually this method is combined with a literal interpretation of the numbers in Revelation. For example, the thousand-year reign (20:1-6) is taken as so many calendar years—despite the symbolism that is so clearly intended by the author. Did John have no message for his immediate audience? Did God inspire him to write a puzzle which nobody could decode until our time? If there is a meaning for us today, there must be a better way.

2. Revelation is talking about events and persons of the AUTHOR'S time. This would seem to be obvious. It is one of the methods used by all serious scholars today. Using the historical-critical approach, they try to determine the author, the life-situation, the intended audience, the sources John may have used, and, above all, his aim or intention in writing the book. Their conclusion is that John was writing toward the end of the first century for the churches of Asia Minor, which were faced with persecution from the Roman authorities.

His vision of the immediate future concerns the fall of Rome—which is the Beast, the instrument of Satan—soon to be "bound" for a long period of time (the thousand-year period). After that he will be released for a final battle and then sent to the fiery pool forever, along with the wicked. Meanwhile the faithful will be granted eternal life. Thus, while there is a *general* timetable for the distant future, there are only markers for its beginning and end. However, the immediate future, the great tribulation about to begin, is described in great detail (though figuratively), with many replays of Old Testament plagues.

The historical-critical method emphasizes the *distance* between the modern reader and the author. But if the church reads this book as God's ongoing Word, how do we hear what Revelation is saying to us *now*? However valid and necessary the historical-critical method is, there must be something more to complete the "hermeneutical circle."

3. What Revelation said THEN also speaks to us NOW: the Analogical Method. This method respects the historical-critical method and fully uses its resources. What John intended to say thus exercises a control upon our possible interpretations. Otherwise, "if there are no limits on the possible interpretations of the beast in Revelation, a human group, such as the Jews, can be victimized more easily and with apparent biblical sanction" (Adela Y. Collins). The original meaning eliminates certain options. For example, if we believe that the ultimate human value is the preservation of human life, we can hardly find justification for that position in Revelation, which extols the value of martyrdom.

From the original meaning of the author, we can derive a meaning for our day, not by a literal and arbitrary transferral, but by a prayerful, Spirit-guided listening to both the text and to our contemporary experience. We study the text, taking the situation and the intention of the author seriously. Then we study, pray, and share in a community of faith and scholarship to seek the *similarities* and the *differences* between the time and situation of the author and our own.

For instance, how do we living in a culture that is nominally Christian, where the church is not openly persecuted and is guaranteed freedom and rights, hear texts written in a time of persecution? Our culture is really post-Christian. The church is battered by anti-Christian values. If our problem is not persecution, is it perhaps seduction? Seduction is an important theme of Revelation. Thus we can find *analogies* to our contemporary situation in this book, not merely in the sense that "history repeats itself" but because God's Word challenges us in *our* situation just as it did in *theirs*. In Revelation the calamities and plagues which God allows are warnings and appeals to conversion. The time is prolonged in order to give more people a chance to turn from their wickedness. We can see in the local and worldwide conflicts and tribulations of our day the same kind of call to conversion, not only of "others" but of ourselves as well.

Is this an abuse of the text? Does it go against the intention of the author? Hardly. For one thing, John himself resurrects many images from the biblical past, even some from contemporary popular history (e.g., Nero) or mythology (e.g., the woman and the Dragon). He makes montages of them and projects them upon the screen of his day to *interpret* persons or events within the immediate or imminent experience of his readers. This suggests that the same drama God was doing in the past is being played out again in John's day. This justifies our using John's imagery to discover how that drama is being lived out in our day. But for this, we need the light of the Holy Spirit and a discernment full of respect for the nature of the book we are studying. The commentary and the material for reflection, prayer, and study are intended to assist that process.

THE VALUE OF SHARING

The community of faith in which we seek the meaning of Scripture is another protection against subjective or arbitrary interpretations. For this reason, sharing with other faith-filled Christians is one of the best ways to get at the *Now* meaning of this text. For Catholic Christians, the "community of faith" also means the universal church—that community extending in space throughout the world and in time, back to the apostolic age and "persevering in the teaching of the apostles" (Acts 2:42) mediated through the "magisterium," the teaching authority of the church.

As long as we are humbly open to having our personal interpretations corrected, there is no danger that the Word of God that we prayerfully study and share will be anything other than the nourishment he tells us it is (Dt 8:3). Hence, Bible sharing or study in a parish or religious community can be an ideal vehicle for understanding and applying the message of a book like Revelation.

A final practical note: You will find that references to modern authors and their books are abbreviated in parentheses. For complete information refer to the bibliography.

PART ONE

✧ ✧ ✧

Setting the Stage

ONE

Introducing the Narrator and the Son of Man
(1:1–1:20)

ALL SCRIPTURE POINTS TO Jesus, for even the old law was prophecy (Mt 11:13). In Jesus all the promises of God are fulfilled (2 Cor 1:20). God, who spoke in times past through the prophets, has now spoken to us in his Son (Heb 1:1-2). The Apocalypse, the last book in our Bible, is to be read as "the revelation of Jesus Christ" (1:1). The opening chapter presents Jesus as the "Son of Man," the risen Lord and Messiah now reigning in his Father's glory. We are thus invited to read the entire book as a personal message from Jesus. He reveals not only the Father. He reveals not only what was happening or about to happen to the seven churches. He also reveals the meaning of the ongoing events of our lives.

OPENING SCENE

¹The revelation of Jesus Christ, which God gave to him, to show his servants what must happen soon. He made it known by sending his angel to his servant John, ²who gives witness to the word of God and to the testimony of

Jesus Christ by reporting what he saw. [3]Blessed is the one who reads aloud and blessed are those who listen to this prophetic message and heed what is written in it, for the appointed time is near. Revelation 1:1-3

❖ ❖ ❖

The first word of this book sets it apart from every other book of the New Testament and from most of the books of the Old Testament: *Revelation* (*apokalypsis* in the Greek, from which comes the more literal translation "apocalypse"). All of the Bible, of course, is presented as revelation and is taken as such by the church. But here the word refers to a particular kind of literature which became increasingly common in Judaism in the last two centuries before Christ and in the first century after Christ. The term *apocalyptic*, which scholars have given to this type of writing, was taken from the opening title of John's book.

The reader will quickly notice the great differences from the Gospels and the New Testament epistles. Here visions abound; so do symbolic numbers and animals, combinations of metaphors almost to the point of incoherence at times, and a preoccupation with the future—all is presented as a direct revelation to John, who also calls this work a "word of prophecy." From it we can get some idea of at least one form of prophecy in the early church. In discussing the prophetic gifts, Paul had already spoken of them as "a revelation" (1 Cor 14:26). We have no way of knowing whether the form of what Paul described as "revelation" resembled what we find here.

In any case the revelation is given by God, first to Jesus, then to "his servants." Jesus is the prime revealer of the mystery of the future. It is he whom John first sees in a vision (1:10-20). It is he who will break open the seals (Chapter 5). However, this is in contrast to the Gospel of John, where the revealer of the things to come is the Holy Spirit (Jn 16:13), and Paul, where revelation and the other prophetic ministries are gifts of the Spirit (1 Cor 12-14). John receives the revelation from Jesus through the ministry of an angel. Later we will see that more than one angel is involved.

This chain from God to Jesus to the angel(s) and to the seer (prophet) echoes late Judaism's increasing tendency to preserve the transcendence of God by introducing intermediaries. It is strange that the "Holy Spirit" does not appear anywhere in the Book of Revelation as the revealing spirit, except in the veiled image of the river of life flowing from the throne of God and the Lamb (22:1), or as the inviting and longing spirit (22:17). Is this because the image of an angel gives a more immediate experience of personhood in the revealer? In other words, does it put some kind of face upon the spiritual movement in the seer that results in a vision? We can only speculate.

Perhaps it would be helpful to note that the Johannine notion of the Holy Spirit as *paraclete* was probably arrived at by transferring an angelic function to the Holy Spirit. This is the case with the idea of the archangel Michael as developed in the Qumran writings (see George Montague, *The Holy Spirit: Growth of a Biblical Tradition*, pp. 321-32, 349-65).

Who are the "servants" whom the author describes as the final beneficiaries of this revelation? We would normally think of the book's entire Christian audience. However, "servants" is also used in Revelation in a more restricted sense to mean the "prophets." These are members of the community who are recognized as having prophetic gifts so outstanding that they occupy some kind of official status, such as John himself. Surely John's message is meant primarily for the prophets among his listeners, but also through them to the entire church.

"What must happen soon" is an expression taken (as is so much of John's vocabulary) from Daniel 2:28. In Daniel, the imminent event is the end of four tyrannical empires and the establishment of a new empire under the Lord's kingship. Here it could refer to the entire progression of history to its end with the final coming of Christ. It is much more likely that John heralds something more limited and immediate: a new persecution of the church about to begin, with its consequences both of suffering and of conquest. John bears witness to the Word of God (1:2). It probably means not the whole of revelation but God's imminent purpose, as in Isaiah 55:11, where the Word that goes forth from God achieves the end for which it is sent. John is testifying not only to that purpose but to the "testimony of Jesus Christ." This could mean the revelation that the glorified Jesus is giving to John. But the Greek word *martyria,* meaning witness, also evokes the witness Jesus gave before Pilate and on the cross—a witness to which many of his followers will now be called in the great persecution. Jesus was faithful to his mission of revelation even unto his death. Thus he is the first martyr.

The prologue concludes with a double blessing (1:3), the first of seven "beatitudes" that grace Revelation (1:3; 14:13; 16:15; 19:9; 20:6; 22:7,14). In a culture where few people could read and most communication was oral, one who could read aloud to the entire community was especially appreciated. "Reading" was what one did "into the ears" of others (Jer 36:6, 10, 14). Here the one who does that receives a special blessing from the Lord. But the hearers are equally blessed, even those unable to read. For revelation is made "to the ears" (Jer 2:2; Ez 8:18; 9:1; 1 Sm 9:15). Obviously, we are in a liturgical setting, not unlike our gathering today to hear the Word of God. That Word has the power not only to enlighten but to convert and to heal.

In 1990 Luz Escobedo of El Paso, Texas, told me that ten years earlier, she was suffering from a calcification in her heels so severe she could hardly walk. She came to a conference. After listening to me proclaiming the Word of God, she immediately stood up, put all her weight on her heels, and walked without pain. She has never experienced pain in her heels since.

At a similar conference at Biscayne College in Miami in the early 1970s, a man named Gus (I do not know his last name) was completely deaf in one ear and half-deaf in the other. He experienced a complete healing while listening to me proclaim the Word of God. But the credit goes not to me but to the Word of God I was proclaiming. For Gus the blessing of Revelation was fulfilled literally: "Blessed are those who *hear* the word." He heard and was healed.

To hear biblically also means to *do* the Word, to move where it calls. The blessing is promised to those who *obey* the Word, not to the idle listener (Mt 7:24-26; Jas 1:22-25). John meant his blessing for the immediate readers and listeners in the seven churches. Surely he intended it to extend to any of his contemporaries who would open themselves to its message. And what of us today? The blessing is still available to those who listen with a believing and obedient heart.

What is the "appointed time" that is "near"? Paul spoke of the nearness of the "time" to exhort his readers to a holier, more fervent living of the Christian life (Rom 13:11; 1 Cor 7:29). At the end of Revelation Jesus says, "I am coming soon" (22:7). Does John understand this to be the final coming in glory at the end of time? Or does he mean Christ's coming imminently in the cross of persecution and martyrdom? The disciples expected an imminent, triumphant coming of Jesus (Lk 17:20-21; Acts 1:6), but they were asleep when he came to them in the passion (Mk 14:40, 43, 45). John—who is about to describe the great tribulation before the final consummation—means Jesus' coming in the cross, although he may also be thinking of the final glory of that sacrifice.

It is often the sudden realization of the brevity of life that awakens us to the really important things. In September 1977, a 727 passenger jet was approaching the San Diego airport when it was struck by a small two-passenger training plane. Months later I read the transcript of the cockpit tape which recorded the sixteen seconds between the collision and the crash. The first words, of course, were questions about what had happened and then a review of options in an attempt to get control of the plane. When finally it was obvious that death and disaster were imminent, the final voice on the tape said, "Ma, I love you."

My mother's last days were spent in an oxygen tent with a tracheotomy which prevented her from speaking. Although she could hear perfectly, she could communicate only with the help of a pencil and writing tablet. As she became weaker even the writing became problematic. A few days before she died, she asked for the writing tablet and made a heroic effort to write something. But her strength failed her. Instead, she just pointed to her heart and then to us. It was April 1974, the month when our family's overdue tax reports should have been filed. Since my mother was the one who did the family accounting, I asked her if she was worried about filing the returns.

She gave me a look of disgust that said, "Who would worry about that at a time like this?" I now know for certain what she was trying to write on that tablet. It was the words, "I love you." I have often wondered how I could have been so preoccupied with the transient—so unaware of the true meaning of the time left to her and us, that I could miss the most important message of her life! What a grace it is to realize *the time is short!*

OPENING SPEECH

[4]John, to the seven churches in Asia: grace to you and peace from him who is and who was and who is to come, and from the seven spirits before his throne, [5]and from Jesus Christ, the faithful witness, the firstborn of the dead and ruler of the kings of the earth. To him who loves us and has freed us from our sins by his blood, [6]who has made us into a kingdom, priests for his God and Father, to

7- used 50 times in Revelation
wholeness, perfection)

him be glory and power forever [and ever]. Amen.
⁷Behold, he is coming amid the clouds,
   and every eye will see him,
   even those who pierced him.
All the peoples of the earth will lament him.
   Yes. Amen.
⁸"I am the Alpha and the Omega," says the Lord God, "the one who is and who was and who is to come, the almighty."   Revelation 1:4-8

✧ ✧ ✧

From the way John addresses his audience, we expect this book to be a letter. He follows the Greek letter-writing style of the day and moreover he uses Paul's familiar greeting, "Grace and peace." From Chapter 4 onwards, however, the contents look like anything but a letter. The bulk of his work is an apocalyptic prophecy, similar to those contemporary Jewish works which were usually said to have remained hidden or sealed up for generations but now have been discovered.

But John does not want his work to be secretive. Nor does he want it to be hailed and divulged as an ancient document only recently discovered. John wants his message to be read publicly in all the churches, just as were Paul's letters. He concludes the book as he would a letter (22:21). This epistolary framework sets his book apart from other apocalyptic works: it is a prophecy wrapped in a letter.

By addressing it to the "seven churches in Asia," John anticipates his enumeration of them in 1:11 and the actual letters in Chapters 2 and 3. There were surely other Christian communities in Asia. He selects seven, perhaps because that number is highly symbolic for him, but perhaps also because seven, representing totality, might suggest all the churches of Asia Minor.

Though each church enumerated in 1:11 will receive a particular message, John consigns all seven letters to a single work to be widely circulated. Thus he implies that each community had something to learn from the message addressed to the others. John gives no key as to how the Ephesians, for example, should apply the letter to Sardis to their situation, but he assumes they will do so. This provides us with a clue and an authorization to apply these ancient letters to our situation today. It enables us to find in them a fresh Word of God. The visions from Chapter 4 onwards, of course, are meant for all the seven churches.

Being a Jewish author, John prefers to speak of the transcendent God in indirect ways. Thus God is "he who is and who was and who is to come" (1:4). We might have expected "will be" instead of "to come." The latter phrase, however, makes it clear that this God is not living in some blissful but disinterested eternity. Rather he is going to *enter* into human history in some way—specifically in the ways that John is about to detail in his book.

Adding "the seven spirits before his throne," particularly before the mention of Jesus, is surprising. Perhaps John puts Jesus in third place for practical reasons, that is, he wants to give a longer description of who Jesus is. This section would have been clearly Trinitarian if John had spoken of "the Spirit" (singular) instead of the seven spirits. Here again we come upon the mysterious pneumatology of Revelation. John was surely aware of the tradition about the Holy Spirit. But he also wants to show the dynamic and versatile nature of God's spiritual activity.

Describing this dynamism as seven spirits allows him to convey not only perfection and unity (the number seven) but also the dynamism of mission. Jesus is portrayed as the Lamb, the one who died and yet lives—thus evoking his earthly mission. So the "spirits" evoke not only their facing God but the various earthly ministries that they will exert. Though Paul knows what may be the older tradition when he speaks of the "spirits [plural] of the prophets" (1 Cor 14:32), he considers these to be ministries or gifts of the one Spirit (1 Cor 12:4). John, more in keeping with the pneumatology we find in the apocalypses, describes them as seven spirits.

They are not, however, above Christ, for as we shall see in 3:1, like God himself he has the seven spirits. These spirits are apparently angels, for the stars which Christ holds in his hand are identified as the angels of the seven churches (1:16, 20; 2:1).

Jesus is described with three titles and three activities (1:5-6). The titles come from John's rich store of scriptural images of the Messiah, all of them taken from Psalm 89. He is first "the faithful witness." In Psalm 89:38, God's promise to David that his kingship will last forever is like the moon, a "faithful witness in the sky." Here it is not a symbol from nature but the person of Jesus himself, who is the faithful witness (the fulfillment of *all* God's promises, see 2 Cor 1:20). By his own fidelity to God unto the cross, he bore witness to God's fidelity. Now he shines not in the physical sky but in the resurrected glory of heaven.

In that same psalm, God makes his Messiah "the firstborn" (Ps 89:28). In ancient Israelite society, the firstborn succeeded the father as head of the household, having authority over his brothers and sisters (Gn 27:29, 37). The firstborn was also consecrated to the Lord and had to be "redeemed." In other words, the firstborn was returned to the parents through sacrifice (Israel's way of doing what other nations often did by offering human sacrifice).

When applied to the king upon his enthronement, the image meant God's adoption of the ruler as his son ("I will *make* him the firstborn"). God endowed him with full authority not only over the nation but also over all the other kings of the earth. Here in Revelation, however, Jesus is firstborn of the *dead*. He is the first to experience the resurrection which will eventually be conferred upon all those faithful until the end. But the idea of kingship and rule is also in the background, for Jesus' resurrection is his enthronement as Messiah and Lord (Acts 2:36). If he is the firstborn, others who have died in him will follow to share his glory and reign.

Already in Psalm 89 the Lord promises that he will make the firstborn, the Messiah, highest of the kings of the earth (Ps 89:28). So here it is natural to add that Jesus is "ruler of the kings of the earth." Commentators have remarked how preposterous such an affirmation was in the face of the reality of the Roman Empire. Yet such is John's faith that Christ is not king merely of a heavenly empire, but also the "King of Kings" (19:16) here on earth. The Book of Revelation is not a program for "pie in the sky" Christian living nor for escape from the political realities of the earth. God intends Christ to rule on earth, as Christians prayed since Jesus taught them the words, "Thy kingdom come, Thy will be done *on earth* as it is in heaven."

The three titles are followed by three actions of Christ. He *loves* us. Note the present tense. For those about to be led to the slaughter it would not be sufficient to say with Paul, "He loved me" (Gal 2:20). However true and consoling the memory of Calvary might be, the question before the martyr-candidates was surely whether Christ loved them *now*, in *their* calvary.

Should not the one suffering of Christ be sufficient to liberate his followers from all suffering? Or at least from the ultimate suffering of martyrdom? Are we not resurrection people? Do we not live in glory already now? And if God loves us, why do we suffer? John does not answer that question here. He merely affirms, as does Paul, that one can be victorious *in* suffering because of him who loves us (Rom 8:37-39).

One week after returning from Medjugorje a high school student in Louisiana suffered a near-fatal accident which put him in a back brace and forced him to miss a year of his schooling. I wondered how he interpreted the event in the light of his recent pilgrimage, for it certainly did not appear to be a blessing. "Oh," he answered, "but it was my experience of the Lord's love at Medjugorje that enabled me to bear the burden even with joy."

Jesus' present love is founded in what he has already done. The new exodus has been marked by the shedding of blood, that of the eschatological Paschal Lamb. His blood has sealed those marked for escape from the Egypt of sin. John does not say that Christ *redeemed* us by his blood, instead that he *freed* us. The choice of this word is very meaningful in the light of the suffering Christians are already enduring. The real liberation has already happened! They may be behind iron bars, and the shadow of the sword may already be falling across their brow. Yet Jesus has already broken the bars and the chains of sin, selfishness, greed, lust, and bitterness.

Like Thomas More, Dietrich Bonhoeffer, and all Christians who clung to their conscience before a tyrant's threats, they experience freedom where it really counts: in the mind and heart. I once visited a young man in prison because of his witness to Christian values. I expected him to complain about his life in jail. Instead he said he was living in luxury compared to the poor he had worked with, especially the babies who were being destroyed in their mothers' wombs. As I listened to him talk, I wished *I* had the freedom he had.

The freedom Jesus gives is not merely a freedom *from*. It is a freedom *for* (1:6). When the Lord, having delivered his people from Egypt's bondage, made a covenant with them, he said, "You shall be to me a kingdom of priests, a holy nation" (Ex 19:6). The kingdom, of course, will be that over which the Lord presides as king. But what does it mean to be a "kingdom of *priests*"?

Priests represent others before God and mediate God's blessings to them. All of Israel will fulfill this role of religious mediation for the rest of the world. The other nations may not know the true God but Israel does. In living out the covenant it will, like Abraham, be a source of blessing for the nations (Gn 12:3). Within Israel, the priestly tribe had no land of its own but was supported by the other tribes in return for priestly service. In a similar way, the nations will, unwittingly no doubt, pour their wealth into Israel.

The Book of Isaiah foretold: "You yourselves shall be named priests of the Lord, ministers of our God you shall be called. You shall eat the wealth of the nations and boast of riches from them" (Is 61:6). The writer of Revelation knew that this was hardly fulfilled in historical Israel, since Jerusalem and the temple lay in ruins. But he sees the prophecy fulfilled in the Christian community.

Perhaps he is even hinting that just as the levitical priests had no land of their own, the persecuted community may be dispossessed. However, the day will come when they will inherit the earth (Ps 37:11; Mt 5:5). He will say as much of the martyrs in 20:6. Here it is all Christians who are envisaged as priests, offering with and in Christ their lives and the world to God, and mediating the divine blessings.

Christians entered their royal priesthood at baptism (1 Pt 2:9). "His God and Father" is a typically Christian title. The Lord's new covenant is also the revelation of the face of God in a way unimagined in the Old Testament: God, yes, but now the God and Father of Jesus Christ. In the fourth Gospel Jesus tells Mary Magdalene to tell his disciples, whom he now calls *brothers*, "I am going to my Father and your Father, to my God and your God" (Jn 20:17). The Christian priesthood of all believers is, therefore, a ministry with and in Jesus, to the God now fully revealed in him.

The titles and the actions of Jesus are concluded with a doxology—a proclamation of glory. It is to Jesus, rather than explicitly to the Father, that this short acclamation of praise is addressed. He is the subject of both what precedes and what follows. This is the first of many liturgical choruses that will periodically conclude a unit or intentionally interrupt the flow of the narration in Revelation.

A new hymn appears in 1:7, using elements of Old Testament theophanies. Daniel says that he saw "one like a son of man coming on the clouds of heaven" (Dn 7:13). The "son of man" there is a collective figure for the "holy ones of the Most High" (7:18), that is, faithful Israel. But already in the apocalyptic Book of Enoch, this figure was interpreted as an individual, the heavenly Messiah-Judge who would inaugurate God's kingdom on earth. (The Book of Enoch is a work of the second century B.C. and not part of the canon, but important enough to be quoted in the letter of Jude 14-15.)

John, who will soon have a vision of this "one like a son of man" (1:13), uses this imagery to evoke the coming of Jesus in glory, adding that "every eye will see him." The word *see* connects this image of Danielic origin to the second Old Testament allusion drawn from Zechariah 12:10. There the prophet foretells the time when his people will repent for having slain a true prophet. "They shall look on him whom they have thrust through, and they shall mourn for him as one mourns for an only son, and they shall grieve over him as one grieves over a firstborn."

The author of the fourth Gospel saw this prophecy fulfilled when Jesus' side was pierced with a lance (Jn 19:37). Here the prophet of Revelation states that it will be fulfilled at the coming of Christ in glory. As in the Gospel of John (Jn 20:27) so here the Risen One bears the wounds he received (he is the "slain Lamb," 5:6), wounds that are now available as sources of healing (Is 53:5; 1 Pt 2:24).

One day they will be the evidence of condemnation for those who refused the grace of mercy. It is not only those who pierced him who shall mourn, nor all the tribes of Israel (the view of Zechariah 12:11-14), but all the peoples of the earth—those who, in view of the proclamation of the gospel to the whole world, will have had an opportunity to accept or reject the message of salvation.

This introductory section concludes with a direct word from "the Lord God, the Almighty" (1:8). The title is the Greek rendering of *YHWH elohe sabaoth,* sometimes rendered "the Lord, the God of hosts" in our translations (Hos 12:6; Am 9:5). It is a title particularly dear to John; it reveals his thorough Jewishness. It stresses the transcendence, power, and authority of Israel's God who speaks. To the previous description of the Lord as "the one who is, who was and who is to come," which we commented upon in 1:4, the text here adds, between "Lord God" and "Almighty," the title "the Alpha and the Omega" (the first and the last letters of the Greek alphabet).

God is the beginning and the end of all, the first and the last—an image that will run throughout the Book of Revelation (1:17; 2:8; 21:6; 22:13). It will even appear in thousands of Christian churches in later ages. Presently it is used in the Catholic Easter Vigil when the presider blesses the Paschal candle, a symbol of the risen Christ. Cutting a cross into the candle with a stylus, he inscribes the Alpha above the cross and the Omega below it, then marks the current year, saying, "Christ yesterday and today, the beginning and the end, Alpha and Omega. All time belongs to him and all the ages, to him be glory and power through every age forever. Amen."

At this point in Revelation, however, it is to God (the Father) that these attributions are made. Later they will be applied to Christ.

INTRODUCING THE SON OF MAN

⁹I, John, your brother, who share with you the distress, the kingdom, and the endurance we have in Jesus, found myself on the island called Patmos because I proclaimed God's word and gave testimony to Jesus. ¹⁰I was caught up in spirit on the Lord's day and heard behind me a voice as loud as a trumpet, ¹¹which said, "Write on a scroll what you see and send it to the seven churches: to Ephesus, Smyrna, Pergamum, Thyatira, Sardis, Philadelphia, and Laodicea."

¹²Then I turned to see whose voice it was that spoke to me, and when I turned, I saw seven gold lampstands ¹³and in the midst of the lampstands one like a son of

priesthood   kingship royalty

man, wearing an ankle-length robe, with a gold sash around his chest. [14]The hair of his head was as white as white wool or as snow, and his eyes were like a fiery flame. [15]His feet were like polished brass refined in a furnace, and his voice was like the sound of rushing water. [16]In his right hand he held seven stars. A sharp two-edged sword came out of his mouth, and his face shone like the sun at its brightest.

[17]When I caught sight of him, I fell down at his feet as though dead. He touched me with his right hand and said, "Do not be afraid. I am the first and the last, the [18]one who lives. Once I was dead, but now I am alive forever and ever. I hold the keys to death and the netherworld. [19]Write down, therefore, what you have seen, and what is happening, and what will happen afterwards. [20]This is the secret meaning of the seven stars you saw in my right hand, and of the seven gold lampstands: the seven stars are the angels of the seven churches, and the seven lampstands are the seven churches. Revelation 1:9-20

❖ ❖ ❖

By naming himself as author John parts company with other apocalypses of the time. In those works the writer usually assumed a name of some ancient personage like Abraham or Moses or Enoch in order to lay out the future in historical periods—some of which would have already passed by the time of the writing of the document. In this way the writer would lend plausibility to his prophecies, since part of them would have already been fulfilled. Neither do we find in Revelation the idea of a document that was long lost and only recently found.

Our author is more direct. He is writing prophecy. His authority comes not only from his claim of divine inspiration but also from his suffering with those whom he addresses. He does not speak with detached interest like an impassive counselor. He is their *brother* and, like Jesus, he will speak from within the suffering which he, like them, is experiencing. He is sharing with them three things:

1. the distress;

2. the kingdom;

3. the endurance.

Logically, we would expect the order to be, first the distress (i.e., the objective ordeal), then the endurance which it evokes from the faithful, then the kingdom which it merits. But this placement of the chief element in the middle is not uncharacteristic of a style we find elsewhere in the New Testament. For example, 2 Timothy speaks of "a spirit of power and love and self-control" (2 Tm 1:6). Here the central term "love" is like the fuselage of an airplane borne on balancing wings, since "power" is tempered by "self-control."

In our present text, the "kingdom" is obviously the ultimate in importance, but it is attained when the distress is responded to by "endurance in Jesus." It is precisely to encourage this endurance that the book is written. Perhaps for that reason John places it in the final position.

It is remarkable, however, that it is not just an endurance *for* Jesus but *in* him. The ability to persevere under trial and persecution is possible because, by grace, the faithful experience a union with Jesus. They reproduce his suffering, and in some sense he continues to suffer in them. There is a level of communion with Jesus which is possible only to those who suffer with him.

Patmos is a small island just off the west coast of Asia Minor, some sixty-five miles southwest of Ephesus (see map on page 11). John was probably banished there by the local governor, possibly for his resistance to emperor worship. The martyrdom of Antipas (2:13) shows that persecution has already begun. John has suffered because he publicly proclaimed the gospel and bore *witness* to Jesus. This theme becomes a central one in Revelation.

To be "caught up in spirit" (1:10) recalls the similar expression of Ezekiel (Ez 3:14). It could mean ecstasy or trance, although Paul's use of the term "praying in the Spirit" does not demand such a degree of exaltation (1 Cor 14:15). Because of the intricate literary nature of the book, written on the pattern of Old Testament visionary revelations, some think here the expression is an imitative literary device. In any case John is claiming direct divine inspiration for his message.

By this time the first day of the week is called "the Lord's Day" because it was on this day that Jesus rose from the grave. The Christian practice began in Asia Minor and became commonplace by the end of the second century. John may be intending it here in reaction to the "Emperor's Day," which was instituted as the first day of the month; later it was extended to a day of the week. The Christian Sunday superseded the Jewish sabbath—although in the Roman Empire before Constantine, Christians had to gather before dawn to celebrate the Eucharist, since the secular world did not observe it as a day of rest. Today the church is finding itself increasingly in a similar situation.

A trumpet blast was the customary Jewish way of calling an assembly (Is 27:13; Jl 2:1). It became a signal of God's final gathering of the elect (Mt 24:31; 1 Cor 15:52; 1 Thes 4:16). Here, however, it is like the trumpet blast that announced the theophany on Mount Sinai when God revealed his covenant to Moses (Ex 19:16, 19). The voice itself resembles the instrument; it proclaims a revelation to be publicized to the Christian community.

Since John is told to write the messages on a single scroll for the seven churches (1:11), it appears that a single messenger was to make the rounds of these seven churches (they form a geographical circle in what is today western Turkey), reading out all seven letters to each church. For example, while the community at Ephesus would hear the letter written specifically for it, this church would also hear the messages addressed to the other churches as well. This procedure would reinforce a solidarity among the churches; the praise and admonition given to one would indirectly be a message to all. In the same way, the messages written to ancient churches can also be a message for us today. Some authorities think the seven churches are symbolic of all churches within the reach of John's message.

John not only hears. He sees (1:12). The vision is remarkably similar to Daniel's vision of the heavenly figure in Daniel 10-11 (probably the angel Gabriel, see also Dn 9:21). Other traits are fused from elsewhere in the Bible, and most notably divine traits are introduced. Since the seven-branch candlestick holding seven lamps was made by Moses at God's command for the sanctuary (Ex 25:31-37), John is immediately aware he is in the presence of the All-Holy.

The lamps, however, are more than sanctuary lamps. We are told in 1:20 that they are the seven churches. We are not accustomed to think of our church or diocese as a sanctuary lamp. But on the mount Jesus did say to his disciples, "You are the light of the world" (Mt 5:14). He went on to say that people put a lamp "on a lampstand, where it gives light to all in the house" (Mt 5:15). Here the heavenly mystery of the earthly church is even more: each Christian community is a sign of the presence of the All-Holy God. The lamp is not the individual disciple but the community to which he or she belongs.

"One like a son of man" (1:13) is a direct quotation of Daniel 7:13: the heavenly figure who comes on the clouds of heaven to the throne of God to receive eternal kingship. Explained in Daniel 7:18 as a collective figure for the "saints of the Most High" (i.e., God's people ultimately victorious), this "son of man" was interpreted already in Jewish tradition as an individual, heavenly Messiah (Enoch 46, 48, 62, 69).

By the time John wrote, "son of man" was an accepted title for Jesus, particularly in his second glorious coming to judge the living and the dead. The ankle-length robe marks Jesus as priest (Ex 28:4). The high priest wore a sash. Some of the cloth from which his vestments were made was to be of gold (28:4-5). Though gold also suggests royalty, and Jesus will be named King of Kings later, the emphasis here seems more directly religious or heavenly. In Daniel 10:5 a gold sash is worn by the angel Gabriel.

Standing in the midst of the churches, he is priest, king, and judge. White hair (1:14) describes the "Ancient of Days" (meaning God in Daniel 7:9). Here it is one of many divine traits ascribed to Jesus. Eyes like fiery flame, another image borrowed from Daniel 10:6, means that he sees and knows all. One thinks of the Buddhist stupas in Nepal where two gigantic eyes peer at the visitor wherever he stands. God is the searcher of heart and soul (Ps 7:10). In the light of the judgment on the churches about to unfold, one recalls Jeremiah 17:10: "I, the Lord, alone probe the mind and test the heart, to reward everyone according to his ways."

The feet of polished brass (1:15; see also Dn 10:6) suggest durability. The sound of many waters accompanied the Lord's appearance to Ezekiel (Ez 43:2). Here it is the voice of the heavenly figure himself. Anyone who has visited a thunderous waterfall like Niagara or Victoria or has heard the surf crashing against a rocky shore may have some idea of the image used here.

The stars in the Lord's right hand (1:16) are later explained as the angels of the seven churches (1:20). It was a common Jewish belief that each individual had a guardian angel (see Mt 18:10). In addition, each nation and city was assigned a heavenly patron, and so it is with the individual Christian communities.

The sword coming from the mouth is a daring image of the WORD OF GOD (Heb 4:12; Eph 6:17). This is an image which appears already in Isaiah: "He shall smite the earth with the rod of his mouth" (Is 11:4), and "He has made my mouth like a sharp sword" (Is 49:2). It was also picked up in 2 Thessalonians 2:9, "He will slay with the breath of his mouth." It is significant that God's WORD, by which he created the world (Ps 33:6), is the only weapon he needs against his enemies.

The face that shines like the sun recalls the transfiguration of Jesus (Mt 17:2). Heavenly beings, when seen by humans on earth, shine like the sun (10:1; 12:1); likewise the just who enter the kingdom (Mt 13:43). Like Daniel (Dn 10:7-9), the seer falls to the ground (1:17), convinced that anyone who would see God would die (Ex 19:21; 33:20; Jgs 6:22-23; Is 6:5).

In touching and reassuring him, the heavenly figure reveals his identity—not by a direct name but by metaphors and titles. He is "the first and the last," a title hereafter used always for Christ. Very significant for the theology of Revelation, the Greek word for "last" is not the neuter *eschaton* but the masculine *eschatos*. This means that the end is a not an event but a person, Jesus Christ. He is the "one who lives." Having first passed through death, he now enjoys and gives life eternal (1:18).

I remember once hearing a Nepali Christian, a convert from Hinduism, preach an Easter sunrise sermon on this text. "Our Christian faith is not in myths but in a real historical person who lived and died, Jesus Christ. But he also rose from the dead. There have been thousands of gurus, but they are all dead. Only Jesus is the living one." As Caird (p. 26) has beautifully commented: "Jesus not only burst out of the prison of death; he carried away the keys. His followers therefore need not fear the dungeon of death, for their Lord will release them."

The three parts of Revelation are set out in 1:19: "what you have seen" (the vision of the Son of Man, 1:10-20), "what is happening" (the situation of the churches, Chapters 2-3), and "what will happen afterwards" (the events of Chapters 4-22). It is important to remember that the rest of the book is dominated by this vision of the glorious, living Lord. However much of the book will speak about his *coming*, Jesus is already in the midst of the church speaking his Word both of salvation and of judgment.

✧ ✧ ✧

Reflection

Revelation states that Jesus is the ruler not only of heaven but also of the kings of the earth. He is the Lord of history. This is an amazing, and to some an incredible, claim. For history often seems to proceed on its own course, either ignoring the gospel or following its own gospel, or sometimes opposing the gospel of Jesus Christ. But Christians believe not only that God is the Creator of the universe of matter and spirit but that his providence guides the events of the earth. The awesome gift of human freedom is part of the mystery, for history is also made of the free choices of human beings, and these often conflict with God's plan of love. Yet even the sins of rebellion and weakness find God's response in Jesus, the Redeemer. He entered human history to lead us out of sin back to the heart of the Father. Jesus' resurrection was God's sign appointing him to be the judge of the living and the dead (Acts 17:31). Though often hidden in the present unfolding of history, Jesus prepares his ultimate rule through the ministry of his church. In moments of prayer, in the vision of the ultimate Revealer, the disciple knows the end even now.

Questions

1. Where, when, and why was Revelation written? How did the author write it so the people of his day could understand it? *Patmos (penal colony) where John was deported for being Christian proselytizer. To seven churches. Brother in suffering that they are all suffering that*

2. Who is the prime revealer of the mystery of the future? Who are the servants who are to receive these messages? What does it mean to be a hearer of the Word of God? *Jesus, Prophets [to do] including John. All followers & disciples of Christ. Watch! Live for Christ coming*

3. How is Christ described? What do the elements signify? What are his actions? *Judge. Long robe - symb priesthood golden girdle - royalty full of energy white hair - eternity - permanence wisdom burning eyes - probe minds, hearts prophecies*

4. How has hearing the Word of God changed my life? *More charitable, loving. Act c love,*

5. If I had two more weeks to live, what would I do? *pray - repentance - love*

Prayer

Lord Jesus, I believe that you are the one who has loved me perfectly, that you were pierced on the cross to win for me eternal life. Like your servant John, I kneel before you with a listening heart. Help me to accept your message and, with my brothers and sisters, to be the lamp signaling your presence in our world today.

stand firm – dont give in to
what is evil.

TWO

Introducing the Audience: Letters to the Seven Churches
(2:1–3:22)

T HE LETTERS GIVE A CONCRETE HISTORICAL focus to the vision of the heavenly Son of Man and to the cosmic drama which will follow. They are the most understandable parts of the entire book.

Our own Christian communities, like those of ancient Asia Minor, are often in trouble or in need of reform. Some common traits run through these letters:

1. They recall one of the descriptions of Christ from the inaugural vision.
2. The Lord himself speaks, first to assure the community that he knows their suffering and good works ("I know").
3. Then he indicts the community for its failings (with the exception of Smyrna and Philadelphia).
4. He tells them to repent in view of his imminent coming.
5. He concludes with a warning to heed the message and a promise of victory to the one who is faithful.

The letters, more than any other part of Revelation, resemble Old Testament prophecies. They are less a prediction of future events than a message of encouragement and challenge to the community faced with a moral or religious crisis.

As you read these letters, think of Jesus, the glorious Son of Man and Lord of history, addressing the Christian communities of today and yourself personally. How does the challenge, for example, to rediscover your first love apply to you, to your community? How does the wealth of Laodicea and its complacency challenge you and your community today?

TO EPHESUS: LOSING THAT FIRST LOVE

¹To the angel of the church in Ephesus, write this: *power*

"The one who holds the seven stars in his right hand and walks in the midst of the seven gold lampstands says this: ²'I know your works, your labor, and your endurance, and that you cannot tolerate the wicked; you have tested those who call themselves apostles but are not, and discovered that they are impostors. ³Moreover, you have endurance and have suffered for my name, and you have not grown weary. ⁴Yet I hold this against you: you have lost the love you had at first. ⁵Realize how far you have fallen. Repent, and do the works you did at first. Otherwise, I will come to you and remove your lampstand from its place, unless you repent. ⁶But you have this in your favor: you hate the works of the Nicolaitans, which I also hate.

⁷"'Whoever has ears ought to hear what the Spirit says to the churches. To the victor I will give the right to eat from the tree of life that is in the garden of God.'"

Revelation 2:1-7

Christ is the original victor.

✧ ✧ ✧

Ephesus was the most important port city of Asia Minor (see map on page 11). It was the meeting point of major Roman roads running through Asia Minor, one of them all the way to the Euphrates (in modern-day Iraq). It was the center for the Roman administration of the province of Asia and the seat of the Roman proconsul. With a population of some 250 thousand in New Testament times, it deserved the many inscriptions which call it "the first and greatest metropolis of Asia." Its famous theater seated 24 thousand spectators. Its temple of Artemis was considered one of the seven wonders of the ancient world.

Both theater and temple figure in the story of Paul's ministry in Acts 19. Originally an Asiatic mother goddess, patroness of fertility, Artemis was identified by the Greeks with the Artemis of the Olympian pantheon, the virgin huntress, sister of Apollo. Ephesus was also famous for its gladiatorial games. It was a center for the worship of the Roman emperor, having built a temple to Claudius or Nero, and later to Hadrian and Severus. No doubt the Christian community, established there since the time of Paul, felt the pressure of the city's expectation that all participate in giving divine honor to Caesar.

Why would John address his letter to an "angel" (2:1)? Some scholars have suggested that, since in Jewish apocalyptic thought the heavenly world is a mixture of good and evil much as the earth is, the "angel" would be the guardian angel of the church of Ephesus who needed to hear this message from the Son of Man, who is Lord of the angels. Others have suggested "angel" is a code word for the local bishop. But it is not evident that the title "bishop" was given to the church leader at this time. No such office is mentioned elsewhere in Revelation. Others think that it means the "presiding elder." Still others have pointed out that the office of "prophet" was the forerunner of "bishop," as indicated by the Didache (15:1-2).

This suggestion gains additional plausibility from the fact that John himself is a prophet. Prophecy, especially in apocalyptic literature, was often mediated to the prophet through an angel (as indeed happens in this book; see also Acts 23:9). "Angel" then would be a code word for the recognized prophet-leader of the community, who would be the visible presence of its invisible prophetic-guardian angel.

The speaker, whose description reminds us of the inaugural vision, praises the community for its "labor" (2:2), especially in its resistance to false prophets and its steadfast endurance for the name of Christ (2:3). This is possibly an allusion to members being interrogated about their Christian faith. Those who "call themselves apostles but are not" are probably itinerant missionaries who tried to import into the community the teaching of the Nicolaitans (2:6, which will be discussed in detail later).

At this period the distinction between apostles and prophets was not clear. They are mentioned together in Ephesians 2:20. In the Didache (15:3-6), an apostle who remains too long in the community or who asks for money is called a false *prophet*, indicating that the two terms were interchangeable. Twenty years later Ignatius praises the church of Ephesus for rejecting "heretical" teachers who passed by on their way (Eph 9:1; see 6:2; 7:1; 8:1). (This is Ignatius' letter to the Ephesians, not Paul's.)

Despite its doctrinal purity, the Lord finds that the church has lost its first love (2:4). How strange! It would seem rather that, because of this act of doctrinal fidelity, the church should be applauded for its fidelity to its first betrothal (as in Jer 2:2).

This text has often been interpreted as a challenge to return to the Lord as one's first love. Basilea Schlink relates how this text brought a second conversion in her life: she had become so busy doing the Lord's *work* that she had forgotten the Lord for whom she was working.

However, the vertical dimension of love seems to have

been well demonstrated by the church's doctrinal fidelity. So it seems more likely that the love referred to is fraternal love. It may be that persecution from without caused the love of many to grow cold (Mt 24:12). Or, more likely, the very struggle to establish doctrinal purity led to a judgmental, censorious attitude within the community. While this church displayed doctrinal purity, it lacked inner harmony and love, and so ran the danger of losing its lampstand. Doctrinal purity is important, but it must lead to love. One can be right, but one is *dead* right without love.

The situation can be remedied. But only by way of repentance (2:5): recognition that its present condition is sinful. Not mistaken or inadequate. Sinful. Turning back to the Lord also means recapturing the honeymoon fervor of the community's early days. If that means falling in love with the Lord and the community all over again, so be it. But the authenticity of the return will be judged not by feelings but by works. The context suggests these are the works of love (as in Mt 25:31-46).

The Jesus of Revelation sounds like the Jesus of the Gospels in his admonition to listen (2:7). Though addressed to the Ephesian community, the message is for all Christians ("whoever has ears") and for all the churches. The words, though apparently spoken by the risen Jesus, are attributed to the Spirit, that is, the Spirit of prophecy. Since John has not mentioned the likelihood of martyrdom yet, the "victor" here is anyone who is faithful unto death.

Christian life is a warfare in which the feeblest saint can prove victorious. Perhaps there is an ironic twist here: the Nicolaitans (which literally means "victory over people") are not the real victors. It is those who are faithful under trial. The tree of life is not exactly the same as the river of life (21:6; 22:17). The latter is given without money and without price to everyone who thirsts for it. The tree of life is rather the reward for the battle of life. An early Jewish tradition (Lv 18:11) claimed that the paradisal tree of life would be transferred to the temple in Jerusalem. In 22:2 it grows in the street of the heavenly Jerusalem. Here it grows in the eschatological garden of God, to which Jesus will give the victor access (see Lk 23:43).

This letter then calls us to be faithful to righteous teaching, as well as to recover the early fraternal love which we experienced before problems developed in our relationships. A community can age when it no longer dreams, when it gets lost in secondary goals, when members fight over their little kingdoms of power or status, when hurts are allowed to fester, and when there is no need felt to repent for betraying the original vision. Has this happened in your family, your community, or your church?

TO SMYRNA: A SLANDERED COMMUNITY

8 To the angel of the church in Smyrna, write this:

"The first and the last, who once died but came to life, says this: 9'I know your tribulation and poverty, but you are rich. I know the slander of those who claim to be Jews and are not, but rather are members of the assembly of Satan. 10Do not be afraid of anything that you are going to suffer. Indeed, the devil will throw some of you into prison, that you may be tested, and you will face an ordeal for ten days. Remain faithful until death, and I will give you the crown of life.

11"'Whoever has ears ought to hear what the Spirit says to the churches. The victor shall not be harmed by the second death.'"   **Revelation 2:8-11**

✧ ✧ ✧

Like Ephesus, Smyrna (modern Izmir) was a coastal town with a great theater and was famous for its gladiatorial games. It too was a center of emperor worship. "The first and the last, who once died but came to life" (2:8) is a flash-back to the inaugural vision (1:17-18) and an anticipation of the promise of life in 2:10.

Does 2:9 mean that the Smyrnians are suffering and poor in the midst of a rich city? Or does it mean that their suffering and poverty is actually a spiritual blessing? Though John could hardly mean that poverty and suffering are good in themselves, he probably means that the Smyrnians' fidelity has indeed turned their misery into a blessing. Paul said that, though poor, he had enriched many (2 Cor 6:10). James said, "Did not God choose those who are poor in the world to be rich in faith and heirs of the kingdom that he promised to those who love him?" (Jas 2:5). Those who, like Francis of Assisi, embrace poverty for the love of God find it a spiritual treasure.

Who are the slanderers who claim to be Jews but are not (2:9)? To understand this it is helpful to remember that, though all peoples in the empire were expected to worship the Roman gods (most polytheists found no problem in adding a few gods to their pantheon), it was not so with the Jews. Rome came to terms with them by permitting the Jews to exercise their religion without interference from the authorities and without the obligation to participate in what the Jews considered idolatrous worship. As long as Christians were considered merely a subspecies of the Jewish faith, they enjoyed the same privileges.

But when the Jews expelled them from their synagogues and refused to be identified with the Christians, then the authorities no longer exempted them from this expectation. The slanderers here, then, are most probably Jews who have publicly accused the Christians of being hostile to the state religion. This we know happened in Smyrna at the time of Polycarp. For John, as well as for Paul (Rom 2:28-29), Christians are now the true Jews. Their accusers are the "synagogue of Satan."

For it is indeed Satan who is pulling the strings behind the events (2:10). Some will be imprisoned for a short time ("ten days" is often used in this general sense—Gn 24:55; Dn 1:12, 14). To all, the Lord says, "Be faithful unto death." Is this a prediction that some will be martyred? Possibly. Certainly the martyrs play an important, in fact, a key role in Revelation. John wants all to be prepared for it here.

But one can be faithful unto death through various sufferings short of martyrdom as well. Every Christian in some sense lives the spirituality of martyrdom, whether in fact God calls him or her to physical martyrdom. Martyrdom was held in such high honor in the early church that, after Constantine proclaimed freedom for the Christians, many seemed to regret that their chances of martyrdom had been eliminated. Augustine had to reassure them, "It is not true that the bridge was broken after the martyrs crossed; nor is it true that after they had drunk from it, the fountain of eternal life dried up" (*Serm.* 304, 1-4; PL 38, 1395-1397). What a contrast to the modern world, where covenants are broken for trivialities and certainly not out of fear of death!

To the citizens of a city known for its athletic games, the "crown of life" would evoke the wreath given to the winner. Obviously eternal life is meant here, the image corresponding to the tree of life in the preceding letter. Again, all the churches are invited to listen to the message to Smyrna (2:11). The "second death" was a rabbinic expression meaning eternal punishment. In 20:14, the second death is eternal punishment in a lake of fire. Though the Christian may have to die the first death (physical) as a witness to his faith, he shall never be touched by the second death of eternal punishment. Hence, apostasy is a greater evil than death.

TO PERGAMUM: ALLOWING IDOLATRY

¹² To the angel of the church in Pergamum, write this:
"The one with the sharp two-edged sword says this:

¹³'I know that you live where Satan's throne is, and yet you hold fast to my name and have not denied your faith in me, not even in the days of Antipas, my faithful witness, who was martyred among you, where Satan lives. ¹⁴Yet I have a few things against you. You have some people there who hold to the teaching of Balaam, who instructed Balak to put a stumbling block before the Israelites: to eat food sacrificed to idols and to play the harlot. ¹⁵Likewise, you also have some people who hold to the teaching of [the] Nicolaitans. ¹⁶Therefore, repent. Otherwise, I will come to you quickly and wage war against them with the sword of my mouth.

¹⁷'Whoever has ears ought to hear what the Spirit says to the churches. To the victor I shall give some of the hidden manna; I shall also give a white amulet upon which is inscribed a new name, which no one knows except the one who receives it.'" **Revelation 2:12-17**

❖ ❖ ❖

Though Pergamum was situated north of Smyrna about fifteen miles from the sea, it could be reached by ships plying up the River Caicus. It was an important center for the manufacture of parchment, which derived its name from the city. It was famous for its library, but more so for its cult of Asklepios Soter, the god of healing, patron of the famous school of medicine established there.

If the worship of the emperor flourished in Ephesus and Smyrna, the official center of it was in Pergamum. In 29 B.C., the city had received permission to build a temple to "the divine Augustus and the goddess Roma." Later temples were built to honor Trajan and Severus, a further indication of how these Asian cities vied with one another in promoting emperor worship. Behind the city rose a cone-shaped hill one thousand feet high, home to multiple pagan temples and altars. The "throne of Satan," the place "where Satan dwells" (2:13), may refer to the temple to Augustus, or to the cult of Asklepios (of whom the serpent was the symbol, which John later applies to Satan in 12:9), or to the conical hill, which he would have understood as the enemy of the "mountain of God" (Is 14:13; Ez 28:14, 16), called the "throne of God" in 1 Enoch 25:3.

The Christian community has held fast to the faith— despite the martyrdom of one of its members, Antipas, the only named victim in Revelation. He is called, in the literal sequence of the Greek, "my witness, my faithful one," an expression full of pathos. "Witness" has not yet come to mean "martyr." It would soon come to mean that in Christian vocabulary from its usage in Revelation and its application to those who gave the ultimate witness to Christ.

Yet all is not well in Pergamum. Balaam and Balak are used here as Old Testament figures for the contemporary situation (2:14). In Numbers 31:16 the women of Moab (of whom Balak was king) "are the very ones who on Balaam's advice prompted the unfaithfulness of the Israelites toward the Lord in the Peor affair." The reference is back to Numbers 25:1-3, where the women of Moab seduced the Israelites into fornication, then into offering sacrifices to Baal, the god of Moab.

Similarly here, the Nicolaitans (2:15) have invited the Christians to eat food sacrificed to idols and to practice fornication. The latter expression could mean direct involvement in pagan sensuous worship and festivals. It may simply be symbolic of the infidelity involved in eating meat that had been sacrificed to idols. Paul had dealt with the problem earlier in Corinth (1 Cor 8:7-13; 10:20-30).

Lest we too hastily judge our early Christian brothers and sisters, let us consider the problems they faced. Obviously, there may have been some Christians who had not really converted from their sensuous pre-Christian lifestyles. There were others who faced the dilemma which many Christians today face with their neighbors in non-Christian countries. When you are living in a pagan religious culture, where seasons and holidays rotate around pagan festivals, and when you belong to trade guilds or have friends and neighbors who are celebrating and invite you to join in the festivities as their guest, what do you do? In Pergamum and elsewhere, this was precisely the social vise in which the Christians were caught. Many of them belonged to trade guilds that had their deity-patrons and their special festival days.

I remember once visiting some Tibetan refugee friends in their tent as they were celebrating the Tibetan New Year. They had cookies and sweets on an elevated table in front of the images of the Buddha. Presumably these had been offered to the Buddha earlier in some religious ceremony. They took the sweets and offered me some. In the East it is a serious breach of courtesy to refuse such hospitality. But would this be considered "communion" with a pagan deity? It was a question that troubled me, not because I thought there was anything wrong with the food, but because I did not know what my partaking would mean to the hosts.

It was only later that I resolved my problem of conscience. I considered the acceptance appropriate, because I had not participated in the religious offering (if there had been one). The people knew I was not a Buddhist, but an outsider to whom hospitality was being shown.

That was, indeed, pretty much the way Paul resolved the question in Corinth. If you buy food in the marketplace, even if it has been offered to idols (a question sometimes hard to determine), eat it without question, but do not participate in the pagan religious sacrificial banquets. We are not sure exactly what the situation was in the communities of Asia Minor. However, the social pressure was probably great to enter wholeheartedly into the traditional pagan festivities. Consider how difficult it may have been for a Christian whose spouse was still pagan.

The revealer of Revelation is uncompromising (2:16). The

identity of the Christian faith is assured only when there is a break with the prevailing culture. The Nicolaitans are for syncretism; John and the voice of Jesus will have none of it. The Lord's judgment is none other than his Word, for that is the only weapon he needs. If his Word created the world (Gn 1), if it can shatter rocks (Jer 23:29) and reach to the point where bone divides from marrow and soul from spirit (Heb 4:12), then it can certainly deal with the false teachers of Pergamum. How it will do so, we are not told.

What a challenge to us who get caught rarely in decisions about participation in false worship but often in the seductions of a secular society that offers us rewards for consumerism, for cutting corners, for little white lies, for opportunism at the expense of others, because it's what everybody else is doing. Refusing to flow with the current may not mean martyrdom, but it might mean risking rejection or ridicule.

The reward is twofold (2:17). Manna is, of course, an allusion to the miraculous bread God gave his people in the desert (Ex 16:4). According to 2 Baruch 29:8, manna would again descend from heaven during the messianic kingdom to feed the blessed. That is probably why it is here called "hidden," that is, in heaven. To those who resist the temptation to eat the idol meats is given the reward of tasting the heavenly manna. Note that this may not involve martyrdom, though it will certainly be costly in other ways.

The second reward is the white stone (translated *amulet* in the *NAB*). In the Hellenistic world, a stone was sometimes used as an admission ticket for a royal assembly. In a jury trial a white stone meant a vote of acquittal. Pliny considers a white stone the mark of happiness. Throughout Revelation, white is a symbol of victory. If these symbolisms are behind the use of the figure here, it would mean that the Son of Man gives to the victor acquittal before the judgment of God and admission to the royal feast of happiness.

However, the inscription of the name gives the stone a

further meaning. Whose name is it? In 3:12, the name of God and the glorious Son of Man are inscribed on the victor himself. But does not the Christian by his baptismal consecration already have those names written on him? How then is the name *new*? Perhaps it is in the same sense that Jesus receives a new name, *Lord,* by virtue of his resurrection (Phil 2:11); sharing in the victory of Christ, the one faithful to death will share in his glorious resurrection. But how can this be a *name known only to him* (the victor)? This phrase underlines the intensely personal nature of the glory he will enjoy: "Star differs from star in brightness" (1 Cor 15:41).

Thus the inscription of the divine name of Christ and God means that the light of glory will relate one who is faithful in a unique and intensely personal way to the Father and the Son. Each one who enters heaven will give God a glory that no one else can give. It will involve the unique and personal witness he gave to Christ on earth. But this unique glory will be first of all God's gift to the individual, the reward of being faithful unto death.

TO THYATIRA: TOLERATING A FALSE PROPHET

[18] To the angel of the church in Thyatira, write this:

"The Son of God, whose eyes are like a fiery flame and whose feet are like polished brass, says this: [19]'I know your works, your love, faith, service, and endurance, and that your last works are greater than the first. [20]Yet I hold this against you, that you tolerate the woman Jezebel, who calls herself a prophetess, who teaches and misleads my servants to play the harlot and to eat food sacrificed to idols. [21]I have given her time to repent, but she refuses to repent of her harlotry. [22]So I will cast her on a sickbed and plunge those who commit adultery with her into intense suffering unless they repent of her works. [23]I will also put her children to death. Thus shall all the churches come to know that I am the searcher of hearts and minds and that I will give each of you what your works deserve. [24]But I say to the rest of you in Thyatira, who do not uphold this teaching and know nothing of the so-called deep secrets of Satan: on you I will place no further burden, [25]except that you must hold fast to what you have until I come.

> [26]"To the victor, who keeps to my
>   ways until the end,
> I will give authority over the nations.
> [27]He will rule them with an iron rod.
>   Like clay vessels will they be smashed,
> [28]just as I received authority from my Father. And to him I will give the morning star.
>   [29]"Whoever has ears ought to hear what the Spirit says to the churches.'"   Revelation 2:18-29

Jeremiah 18: 11

✧ ✧ ✧

Some forty miles southeast of Pergamum lay Thyatira (modern Akhisar). Here the emperor was worshiped as Apollo incarnate and as the son of Zeus. Thus the title "Son of God" (2:18), given to Christ here for the first time in Revelation, is probably a hidden polemic against emperor worship in the city. Reference to his feet "like polished brass" may have been suggested by the fact that there was a guild of metallurgists in Thyatira.

The Thyatirans have grown in love (2:19), in contrast to the Ephesians who lost it (2:4). Their fidelity, their service to one another, and their endurance under duress have been greater than ever. But to this praise, which exceeds that given to the other churches, corresponds an even more severe critique (2:20). For the problem of this church is not so much external persecution as it is false teaching.

It comes from a prophetess who seduces Christians and perhaps other prophets ("servants" could mean either) by teaching them to "play the harlot and to eat food sacrificed to idols." The former expression may refer to the sexual immorality into which some of the pagan banquets degenerated. It might be simply a code word for idolatry, equivalent to eating the idol-offerings.

Because Thyatira was a city of guilds, the Christians there were probably much better off financially than their poorer brothers and sisters in Smyrna (2:9). For the same reason they would be all the more subject to pressures from the guilds. The prophetess promotes participation in the pagan festivals. She claims divine inspiration for her teaching. But John calls her a Jezebel, the queen of Israel who was accused of idolatry and witchcraft in 2 Kings 9:22, since she introduced the worship of Baal into Israel.

The false teaching is not coming from itinerant prophets but from prophets and teachers within the community. John has not been able to dislodge them through previous warnings, nor have the community leaders been able to dissuade her (see "she refuses to repent" in 2:21). Though not named specifically, they are probably Nicolaitans. Repentance is still possible, but if it does not happen, she will become ill and her "children" (those who continue to follow her teaching) will suffer intensely (2:22).

The expression in 2:24, "the deep secrets of Satan," which the Nicolaitans claimed to know, can mean one of two things. In a literal sense it could mean that they claim to be spiritual persons who "know" that they could participate in the pagan banquets without being contaminated. Paul had earlier dealt with such pretenses (1 Cor 8:1-11). Or John could be speaking in an ironic sense, saying that although the Nicolaitans claim to know the "deep things of God," an expression Paul uses in 1 Corinthians 2:10—in reality it is the "deep things of Satan." They were, in any case, promoting an early form of gnosticism which would allow them to maintain their faith in Christ (Roman civil religion rarely required creeds), while enjoying a peaceful coexistence with pagan society by participating in pagan practices.

In any culture in which Christians find themselves, they

need to ask, "Have we compromised too much with the prevailing culture?" Thoughtful Christians will ask the same question today.

The concluding promise (2:26-28) echoes the psalm which was considered to be a prophecy of the Messiah. To him the Lord says, "I will give you the nations for an inheritance and the ends of the earth for your possession. You shall rule them with an iron rod; you shall shatter them like an earthen dish" (Ps 2:8-9). Here this promise is transferred to the victor, that is, the Christian who perseveres in Christ's ways until death. We are being prepared for the later description of the earthly reign of the martyrs with Christ (20:4). The reward is union with Christ himself, for he is the Morning Star (22:16).

TO SARDIS: NOT ALIVE, BUT DEAD

[1] To the angel of the church in Sardis, write this:

"The one who has the seven spirits of God and the seven stars says this: 'I know your works, that you have the reputation of being alive, but you are dead. [2]Be watchful and strengthen what is left, which is going to die, for I have not found your works complete in the sight of my God. [3]Remember then how you accepted and heard; keep it, and repent. If you are not watchful, I will come like a thief, and you will never know at what hour I will come upon you. [4]However, you have a few people in Sardis who have not soiled their garments; they will walk with me dressed in white, because they are worthy.

[5]"'The victor will thus be dressed in white, and I will never erase his name from the book of life but will acknowledge his name in the presence of my Father and of his angels.

⁶"'Whoever has ears ought to hear what the Spirit says to the churches.'" **Revelation 3:1-6**

✧ ✧ ✧

Thirty miles southeast of Thyatira lay Sardis, today a ruin but once the capital of Lydia and famous for its wealthy king Croesus (560-546 B.C.). The earliest known coins originated here in the seventh century B.C., lumps of silver stamped with images of Lydian kings. In the Persian period it was the terminus of Darius the Great's Royal Post Road from Susa (in today's western Iran). Sardis' citadel, thought to be impregnable, was twice taken by surprise, first by the Persian Cyrus in 549 B.C. Later in 218 B.C. a Cretan mercenary climbed the hill and stole unobserved into the fortification, opening the city to the Greek Antiochus. The memory of these events is possibly alluded to in John's warning to be watchful (3:3). In A.D. 26 Sardis competed with ten other Asian cities for the right of building a temple in honor of the emperor. Even though it lost out to Smyrna, the competition attests to the degree to which Asia Minor was enthusiastic for emperor worship.

Of the earlier titles of Christ, John focuses on the seven spirits (1:4) and the seven stars (1:16, 20), which are the angels of the seven churches (3:1). They represent the dynamic element in the hand of Christ, a striking contrast to a church that is dead. For the first time a letter begins without a compliment. The church only appears to be alive. It is not a handful of old people, for when touched by the Spirit, they can dream dreams and prophesy (Acts 2:17-18). Comfortably ensconced in the surrounding culture, it appears hardly Christian enough to merit persecution. John levels against it the harshest criticism yet made of any community: it is dead. And yet not entirely so, for there is something dying that can yet be saved and strengthened (3:3). We are not told what this is. Perhaps the solution to recover life now as then is to get in touch with our original conversion experience, the time when we first heard the gospel (1 Thes 1:5-6; 2:13).

It is a call to a second honeymoon. I once read of a couple who each year on their wedding anniversary would go back to the drugstore where they first met by chance and reenact the scene: she dropping a magazine and he picking it up. It was an annual celebration of that "love at first sight," the magic of which they never wanted to lose. The key to new life for a community is the same. If our community is indistinguishable from the surrounding secular world, it is, as a church, "dead." Life for us, as for Sardis, means going back to our roots.

If Sardis does not recover, the community will experience what its home city experienced on two occasions: being captured by surprise. However, there is even now a faithful nucleus (3:4). To wear soiled clothes in worship was considered a dishonor to God. The white garment, mentioned here for the first time, is a symbol of victory, perhaps even of resurrection. In 2 Corinthians (2 Cor 5:1, 4) Paul describes the glorified life as being clothed from on high. In the *Ascension of Isaiah* 4:16 (around A.D. 80-100) we read: "But the saints will come with the Lord with their garments which are now stored up on high in the seventh heaven; with the Lord they will come whose spirits are clothed... and be present in the world."

In Exodus 32:32-33, the Lord tells Moses he has inscribed the names of those who belong to the community in a book. Those who are unfaithful he will blot out. This book is called "the book of the living" in Psalm 69:29 because it guarantees the blessings to be given to the covenant people. To be blotted out of this book meant to be excluded from the community and its blessings. Later, in the atmosphere of persecution, Daniel uses the term for the first time to refer to the faithful who are destined for immortality (Dn 12:1). That is also the meaning here (3:5). The reward is further described in language that recalls Matthew 10:32: "Everyone who acknowledges me before others I will acknowledge before my heavenly Father."

TO PHILADELPHIA: THE REWARD OF ENDURANCE

[7] To the angel of the church in Philadelphia, write this:
"The holy one, the true,
who holds the key of David,
who opens and no one shall close,
who closes and no one shall open,
says this:
[8]"'I know your works (behold, I have left an open door before you, which no one can close). You have limited strength, and yet you have kept my word and have not denied my name. [9]Behold, I will make those of the assembly of Satan who claim to be Jews and are not, but are lying, behold I will make them come and fall prostrate at your feet, and they will realize that I love you. [10]Because you have kept my message of endurance, I will keep you safe in the time of trial that is going to come to the whole world to test the inhabitants of the earth. [11]I am coming quickly. Hold fast to what you have, so that no one may take your crown.

[12]"'The victor I will make into a pillar in the temple of my God, and he will never leave it again. On him I will inscribe the name of my God and the name of the city of my God, the new Jerusalem, which comes down out of heaven from my God, as well as my new name.

[13]"'Whoever has ears ought to hear what the Spirit says to the churches.'" **Revelation 3:7-13**

❖ ❖ ❖

Twenty-eight miles southeast of Sardis lies the modern Turkish town of Alasehir, the "reddish city" so called for the red hills nearby. In John's day it was called Philadelphia, after its founder Attalus II Philadelphus (159-138 B.C.). In A.D. 17, like many other cities in Asia Minor, it was destroyed by an earthquake, but it was rebuilt with money from the imperial treasury and renamed "New Caesarea." Though apparently still referred to by its old name, the renaming perhaps explains the allusion to the "new name" in 3:12.

Two titles elsewhere applied to God (6:10) and found side by side in 1 Enoch 1:3 and 14:1 are here applied to Christ. He is the Holy One, the True (3:7). Jesus was acknowledged as "the Holy One of God" in Mark 1:24. Holy suggests "otherness"—the transcendence of God or the quality of being set aside for God alone. "True" means not only the quality of speaking the truth but above all fidelity: being true to one's word and one's name, which in biblical terms means loyalty to the covenant relationship. Thus a great act of salvation is about to happen "because of the Lord who is faithful, the Holy One of Israel" (Is 49:7). Here it is Jesus who is faithful to his covenant relationship with his people, those purchased by his blood.

In 1:18 Jesus said he held the keys of death and the netherworld. Here there is one key. It is that of David, an allusion to Eliakim's investiture as master of David's palace: "I will place the key of the House of David on his shoulder; when he opens, no one shall shut, when he shuts, no one shall open" (Is 22:22). Christ holds the keys to the kingdom of God. He has supreme authority in heaven and on earth (Mt 28:18). He is "Son over his own house" (Heb 3:6). The final determination of who enters and who does not is in his hand.

There is surprisingly no negative judgment of this community. On the contrary, not only is the church praised for its fidelity, but it has been successful and will continue to be so in its evangelization efforts (3:8). Such is the common understanding of the "open door," which is used elsewhere for great missionary opportunity (1 Cor 16:9; 2 Cor 2:12; Acts

14:27). Some think the open door is Christ himself (as in John 10:7, 9). That would mean that, although the Philadelphians may be excluded from the synagogue by their fellow Jews, Jesus is the true and only door to the house of God.

Though very modest from a social and political point of view, the community has fulfilled the biblical truth that God chooses the weak to confound the strong (1 Cor 1:27). The difficulty has been a Judaizing group, whom John paints in the darkest colors. They are not the synagogue of the Lord (Num 16:3; 20:4), as they claim to be, but the synagogue of Satan (3:9). The true Jews are now the Christians (Rom 9:6-9; 2:28-29). "They will fall prostrate at your feet": Does that mean that they will be conquered? Or that they will be converted?

In Isaiah 60:10-14 the Lord promised that the gentiles would pour into the new Jerusalem, whose gates would be open day and night, and "they shall fall prostrate at your feet." Ironically, here instead of the gentiles falling at the feet of the Jews, it is the "self-styled Jews" who will fall prostrate at the feet of the Christians (see 1 Cor 14:25). This amazing event will show how much Christ loves them. This echoes another Isaian promise of restoration, which the Lord said he would accomplish "because you are precious in my eyes and glorious, and because I love you" (Is 43:4).

In 3:10 there is a play on the word "kept." Because they have kept Jesus' "message of endurance" (not only his command to endure but his example), he will keep them in the trial about to come on the whole world. For the first time we have a hint of a cosmic trial beyond the confines of the local church. In Chapter 7, the Christians will be sealed as a protection in the great tribulation; we have an anticipation of that here. The coming of Jesus (3:11) probably refers not to his final coming in glory but to his coming in the purging trial soon to be visited on the world. The crown recalls the crown of life promised to the faithful of Smyrna (2:10).

Since there will be no temple in the New Jerusalem (21:22), both "temple" and "pillar" must be figurative here. The allusion may be to those pillars carved in the shape of human figures such as stood in the temple of Artemis in Ephesus or the Erechtheion in Athens. At the time of John's writing, the memory of the earthquake that had destroyed the city in A.D. 17 was still fresh. So was the memory that some citizens had fled the city and continued to live outside it—a fact that would make the promise "he will never leave it" especially meaningful. The city had also been rebuilt and given a new name under Tiberius.

It was a common practice in the period of emperor worship for the local priest, when coming to the end of his term, to erect a statue of himself in the temple area, with an inscription of his name and his father's name. Here Jesus says it is his Father's name (3:12) and his own "new" name (the name "Lord" given him at his resurrection, Phil 2:9-11) that he will inscribe upon whomever has been faithful to the end. Significantly, he will also inscribe the name of the new city, the New Jerusalem (22:2). The author thus uses the historical renaming of Philadelphia to indicate that there is a social dimension to the life of glory, a permanent belonging to the church triumphant. This social dimension balances the intense personal nature of the life of glory, indicated by the new name known only to the receiver in 2:17. Intimacy with God does not exclude, rather it includes community.

Recently the Lord has convicted me of how much my prayer has been preoccupied with *my* struggles, *my* ups and downs, *my* problems, *my* temptations, *my* survival, and how little with the bigger problems of the world and the church. At the same time he seems to be inviting me to take on the preoccupations of the church and the kingdom, which are those of his own heart. More and more I have come to realize that prayer is not talking to Jesus but standing with and in him between the Father and the unfinished work of his kingdom in this world. For in baptism the Lord has called me to have engraved on my heart not only the name of the Father but also the name of the city of God.

TO LAODICEA: LUKEWARM AND COMPLACENT

[14] To the angel of the church in Laodicea, write this:

"The Amen, the faithful and true witness, the source of God's creation, says this: [15]'I know your works; I know that you are neither cold nor hot. I wish you were either cold or hot. [16]So, because you are lukewarm, neither hot nor cold, I will spit you out of my mouth. [17]For you say, "I am rich and affluent and have no need of anything," and yet do not realize that you are wretched, pitiable, poor, blind, and naked. [18]I advise you to buy from me gold refined by fire so that you may be rich, and white garments to put on so that your shameful nakedness may not be exposed, and buy ointment to smear on your eyes so that you may see. [19]Those whom I love, I reprove and chastise. Be earnest, therefore, and repent.

[20]"'Behold, I stand at the door and knock. If anyone hears my voice and opens the door, [then] I will enter his house and dine with him, and he with me. [21]I will give the victor the right to sit with me on my throne, as I myself first won the victory and sit with my Father on his throne.

[22]"'Whoever has ears ought to hear what the Spirit says to the churches.'" **Revelation 3:14-22**

❖ ❖ ❖

Located fifty miles south of Philadelphia and ninety-five miles east of Ephesus, Laodicea was wealthy and had reason to be so. Situated at the convergence of three Roman highways, it was a center for the manufacture of clothing and carpets of native black wool. When it was demolished by earthquakes in A.D. 60-61, unlike other cities it was rich enough to pay for its own rebuilding without applying for an imperial subsidy. It was also home to a famous medical school and an exporter of a prized eye ointment.

These details will be alluded to in the text of this letter. Epaphras, a companion of Paul associated with the Christian community in Laodicea from an early hour (Col 1:7; 4:12-13), may well have been its founder. According to Colossians 4:16, Paul wanted the Letter to the Colossians read to the Laodiceans as well. He also wanted his letter to the Colossians (our present Ephesians?) read in Colossae. (The communities were actually only twelve miles apart.)

Whether by geographical or literary design, the seventh letter occupies the climactic place. The community strangely is not experiencing persecution as the others are. Why is this? Most of its members doubtless belonged to the wealthy merchant class. It appears that they could hardly have remained so, had they not reached some kind of comfortable compromise with emperor worship. If they were still identified as a subgroup of the Jewish faith, they might have enjoyed Rome's exemption of the Jews from such participation. But by this time, given the prevailing situation in the other cities, this is unlikely. If they were still huddling under the Jewish umbrella, their sense of solidarity with the persecuted Christians elsewhere, one of whom had already been martyred (2:13), was highly questionable. The letter zeroes in on what is keeping them from being authentic and fervent Christians: complacency in their wealth.

What is meant by calling Christ the *Amen* (3:14)? Isaiah 65:16 is often translated "God of *truth*," but the original Hebrew text reads literally, "the God of the Amen." The divine title means that God's word is absolutely certain. He says "Amen" to his own blessing or curse. Here is yet another example of a divine title transferred to Christ, whom Paul calls the "Yes" or "Amen" to all the promises of God (2 Cor 1:20). The title here is explained by the following: "the faithful and true witness." It is probably introduced here to challenge the Laodiceans who are unwilling to bear prophetic witness to their faith in the midst of the opulent society with which they have become identified. Caught up with the riches of creation, they have forgotten that Christ is the source of them all.

There is no praise for the church of Laodicea or any individuals in it. Instead, these self-sufficient compromisers with the world are like a lukewarm drink that one spits out (literally, vomits; see 3:15-16). If his people cannot be fervent in spirit (Rom 12:11), the Lord would prefer to have them wrestle with him (cf. Gn 32:23-33) or rebel or fight as Saul had done before his conversion. In that there is energy that can be redirected. But what do you do with people who are spiritually just *blah*?

To ancient Israel's boast, "How rich I have become; I have made a fortune!" the Lord threatened that he would again send them to the desert to live in tents (Hos 12:9). Wealth has created a lack of need—in reality, though, the greatest of spiritual needs (3:17). For the poorest, blindest, and most naked is the one who does not know his need for God.

Christ now bids them buy from him pure gold that is tested by fire (3:18). Fire suggests persecution of the sort other communities have been experiencing. Yet since it is from Christ that they are to buy the gold, it is not necessary that they actually experience persecution, rather that they appropriate the spiritual gold refined in the crucible of Jesus' own passion: Jesus himself.

Then they are to exchange the purple clothes, for which the city was noted, for his white garments of righteousness and victory. A magnificent image for taking a prophetic, countercultural stance! Chameleon-like, you look no different from the pagan rich around you—but if you are Christian, you are different and you should look like it!

As their wealth has made them spiritually blind, they are to seek from Jesus eye ointment infinitely better than that for which the city was renowned. For the reader today, wealth need not be material possessions or money. It can be power, pleasure, achievement, reputation—whatever we make our basic security short of God. Success can be more of an obstacle than failure, if it makes us feel less need for God.

Already the Book of Proverbs (3:12) had said: "For whom the LORD loves he reproves, and he chastises the son he favors." The trials God allows us to experience are signs not of rejection (as nature would have us judge) but of favor (the Greek verb here for "love" in 3:19 is not *agapao* but *philo,* indicating affection). The situation of Laodicea can be remedied through earnest repentance. "Be earnest" translates a form of the Greek verb which implies, "Be zealous and continue in that state, full of fervor" (see Rom 12:11).

The exhortation concludes with a double promise (3:20-21). First, the affection of the preceding verse becomes more specific here. Not only does the Lord threaten, but he comes and seeks entrance into the Christian heart. Notice the deeply personal character of this appeal. In the Gospels Christ invites all to the messianic banquet in heaven (Lk 14:15-24; 22:30; see Is 25:6).

But here there is a double difference: the banquet is now. Christ seeks entry to the believer's home to dine with *him.* There is an echo here from the Song of Songs 5:2: "I heard my lover knocking: 'Open to me, my sister, my beloved, my dove, my perfect one!'" The Lord is not only knocking but calling. "Everyone who belongs to the truth hears my voice" (Jn 18:37), as the sheep respond to the shepherd's voice (Jn 10:3). The promise to enter the believer's house echoes John 14:23: "Whoever loves me will keep my word, and my Father will love him, and we will come to him and make our dwelling with him."

The supper may simply be the celebration of intimate friendship. But a church that regularly celebrates the Lord's supper could hardly miss a eucharistic allusion. Like the disciples at Emmaus, however, who invited their strange companion to dine with them and then recognized him in the breaking of the bread (Lk 24:13-35), the Lord will come to *our* table only if invited.

The second promise (3:21) echoes Luke 22:29-30, where the dining and eucharistic theme also appears. To those who have stood by Jesus in his trials he promises: "I confer a kingdom on you, just as my Father has conferred one on me, that you may eat and drink at my table in my kingdom; and you will sit on thrones judging the twelve tribes of Israel." See also Matthew 19:28 and 2 Timothy 2:12: "If we persevere we shall also reign with him." This promise prepares us for 20:4, where the martyrs are enthroned to reign with Christ for a thousand years.

The situation in Laodicea gives us today reason to pause. There is an almost inevitable connection between wealth and complacency and between poverty and fervor. Recently a retiring Superior General told his religious congregation, "My prayer for our congregation's future is that we have less money and more recruits." A striking story is told of a lax pope in one of the darker ages of the church's history. He had built up his personal wealth and was quite proud of it. In showing a visitor his accumulation, he boasted, "You see, Peter can no longer say, 'Silver and gold I have none.'" To which his visitor responded, "Is that also why Peter can no longer say, 'Arise and walk'?" Wealth is not evil, but wealth that is hoarded numbs one to God and others.

❖ ❖ ❖

Reflection

The churches of Revelation were praised or blamed in relation ultimately to one point: Did they embrace the cross or avoid it? Those who took their faith seriously enough to pay the price of rejection and even persecution were praised and promised eternal rewards. Others preferred to let their faith be suffocated by their chameleon-like absorption of the prevailing culture. In a day when Christian values were more evident in our culture, it may have been easier to live the Christian life. Today we find ourselves in a quite different world. Christian values are not entirely missing, but Jesus' warning to "Watch!"—that is, to discern what is of God and what is not—becomes imperative for those who wish to be faithful and to gain the crown of life.

Questions

1. What are the common traits that run through the letters to the seven churches? *1. description of Christ*

2. "He knows" are sufferings, good works.
3. Indicts for their failings
4. Repent! He's coming soon
5. Warning to heed the message. 6 Victory

2. Why are the messages sent to these seven churches? Who is supposed to read and hear the messages? *Its*

for all Christians ("whoever has ears)

3. Some members of the church of Ephesus, in their struggle for truth, ended up in bitterness toward each other. How do we hate the sin and love the sinner?

Cant be judgmental. Love the Lord 1st! One can be right but one is dead right without love.

4. What does the Greek word *martyrs* mean? How do we live as martyrs today? *Faithful til death.*

"Victor."
Faithful under trial.

5. Which letter to the seven churches applies most to my life today? What can I learn from it?

Prayer

Lord Jesus, if you were writing a letter to me, what would you say? I know that you love me. I know you would find good points in me which you would praise, for they are the work of your grace. Reveal to me, Lord, not only my strengths that you may preserve them but also my weaknesses that you may heal them. Amen.

Its not important what
the future holds!
Its important to know,
who holds the future.

p 95-10 v

The Heavenly Stage: The Immediate Future in Heaven
(4:1–5:14)

N OW BEGINS A DRAMATIC CONTRAST with what has preceded. The letters had come out of a vision, but both vision and letters had been on earth. Now the vision is of heaven. The letters contained threats and promises concerning the future. Some of the future events would depend upon decisions taken in the present. Now we will be given a glimpse of what the future will be like—a future that is not entirely avoidable but one that will confirm, for better or for worse, the faith-decisions made by the Christians in the present age.

We are introduced to an important literary device in Revelation: the split stage or screen. The upper screen describes what is happening in heaven, the lower what is happening or going to happen on earth. These two are intimately related. In Chapters 4 and 5, we are introduced to the heavenly control room, where God and the Lamb are worshiped and where permission is given for the future events to unfold. Here is an important affirmation: though evil and suffering are imminent, the future is in the hands of God and the Lamb.

As we study these chapters, it will be helpful to recall that our liturgies here on earth are a participation in the heavenly liturgy. The prefaces of the Mass frequently recall this fact: "Through Christ the angels of heaven offer their prayer of adoration as they rejoice in your presence forever. May our voices be one with theirs in their triumphant hymn of praise." We too proclaim that God and the Lamb are in charge of history. Before intercession, our first duty, like that of the angels, is pure praise.

THE DIVINE THRONE ROOM

[1]After this I had a vision of an open door to heaven, and I heard the trumpetlike voice that had spoken to me before, saying, "Come up here and I will show you what must happen afterwards." [2]At once I was caught up in spirit. A throne was there in heaven, and on the throne sat [3]one whose appearance sparkled like jasper and carnelian. Around the throne was a halo as brilliant as an emerald. [4]Surrounding the throne I saw twenty-four other thrones on which twenty-four elders sat, dressed in white garments and with gold crowns on their heads. [5]From the throne came flashes of lightning, rumblings, and peals of thunder. Seven flaming torches burned in front of the throne, which are the seven spirits of God. [6]In front of the throne was something that resembled a sea of glass like crystal.

In the center and around the throne, there were four living creatures covered with eyes in front and in back. [7]The first creature resembled a lion, the second was like a calf, the third had a face like that of a human being, and the fourth looked like an eagle in flight. [8]The four living creatures, each of them with six wings, were covered with eyes inside and out. Day and night they do not stop exclaiming:

"Holy, holy, holy is the Lord God almighty,
who was, and who is, and who is to come."
⁹Whenever the living creatures give glory and honor
and thanks to the one who sits on the throne, who lives
forever and ever, ¹⁰the twenty-four elders fall down before
the one who sits on the throne and worship him, who
lives forever and ever. They throw down their crowns
before the throne, exclaiming:
¹¹"Worthy are you, Lord our God,
to receive glory and honor and power,
for you created all things;
because of your will they came to be
and were created." **Revelation 4:1-11**

❖ ❖ ❖

The trumpetlike voice is the same as that of 1:10, the voice
of Christ. Already in the midst of a vision, John is further
"caught up in spirit" (4:2). This probably means he has been
carried through the open door (4:1) into the heavenly throne
room. The Old Testament already considered the heavenly
court to be modeled on that of an earthly king, with the center being the throne (1 Kgs 22:19; Ez 1:26; Dn 7:9). But
since the Holy of Holies in the Jerusalem temple was considered to be the Lord's earthly throne (Is 6:1; Ps 47:8), the
heavenly throne here must also be the heavenly Holy of
Holies. Since God's throne is unshakable, it will stand when
everything else is swept away.

Avoiding anthropomorphic details and even avoiding naming the one on the throne, John describes the scene in terms
of brilliant stones (jasper and carnelian) and the glow of a halo
or rainbow. The rainbow image not only recalls the similar
rainbow in the heavenly vision of Ezekiel (Ez 1:28), but also
the rainbow of mercy given to Noah after the flood. Ancient
peoples thought of the rainbow as the gods' archer-bow. Its
appearance in the sky meant that the gods were appeased.

Going beyond that, the priestly author of Genesis saw the rainbow as the sign of a permanent covenant between God and the earth (Gn 9:12-17). John thus sees not only a sign of the numinous (halo) but also one of reassurance before the chaotic flood of events that will soon follow.

The presence of other thrones and crowns (4:4) is not considered a threat to the single throne and crown. Rather they represent the heavenly council (see Dn 7:9-10). They anticipate the share which the martyrs will have in God's kingdom. Lightning and thunder are traditional effects of theophany (Ex 19:16; Ez 1:13). We have met the seven spirits several times before (1:4,12; 2:1; 3:1). The presence of the sea is of great significance. John has adapted this from the heavenly vision in Ezekiel 1:22-26. But what does it symbolize here? There are three possibilities:

1. A geographical sea, for which there would be many candidates: the Mediterranean, the Sea of Galilee, the Dead Sea, the Nile of Egypt, or the sea of the Exodus. Of these, the last would seem to be the most likely, since it has the most biblical significance.

2. A liturgical sea. In the court of the Mosaic tent, there was a large laver which the priests used to wash their hands and feet before ministering in the tent (Ex 30:17-21). Later in the temple of Solomon, there were ten movable lavers holding some four hundred gallons each and used for washing the sacrifices (1 Kgs 7:27-38; 2 Chr 4:6). In contrast to these the gigantic bronze basin in Solomon's temple, holding some twelve thousand gallons used only for the priests' ablutions, was called the "sea" (1 Kgs 7:23-26; Jer 27:19; 52:20). If such a liturgical sea is meant here, the idea is the necessity of purification before any creature can enter the presence of the all-Holy. Martyrdom could be just such a purification.

3. The mythical sea. In this scene, which is a description of God the creator (4:11), the "sea" would evoke the primeval abyss which God's creative WORD drove into order, by putting some of the waters "above the dome" and the rest "beneath the dome" (Gn 1:7), then further driving the latter into seas (Gn 1:10). Some authors, basing themselves on 2 Enoch 3:3, think the sea of Revelation is the sea that remains above the firmament, i.e., the heavenly ocean (see also Psalm 148:4). This may in fact be the case. However, because this sea becomes the footstool of the martyrs (15:2) and disappears in the new creation (21:1), it must have something to do with the events about to unfold. Thus it must be related to the earthly scene.

In fact the word "sea," even when used of the sea of the Exodus (Ex 15:5, 10), never lost its connection with the primeval abyss (Jb 28:14; 38:16, 30; 41:24; Ps 77:17). It was a reminder of that unspeakable chaos which God drove into order, and which in some way always lurked behind "the sea." If this is the meaning, then the sea here, however crystal clear it might be, represents God's unfinished agenda—the historical chaos such as persecution and martyrdom, through which the faithful must pass but through which they, like their Lord, will emerge victorious (see 15:1-2). *chaos*

In the center on each side of the throne is an animal (4:6). The function of these four animals is not to support the firmament upholding God's throne, as in Ezekiel 1:22-26 and 10:1. Some authors, drawing on contemporary apocalyptic literature, think their function is to guard the throne (1 Enoch 71:7). The only function they have here is the perpetual praise of God (4:8). They therefore most probably represent choirs of angels, with the multiple eyes representing their heavenly knowledge. They see God, but they also know more about earthly things than do humans.

From the time of Ignatius of Antioch (early second century), these figures were identified with the four evangelists. Today in Christian art, the lion represents Mark (his Gospel begins in the desert), the calf Luke (his Gospel begins with Zechariah's sacrifice in the temple), the man Matthew (his Gospel begins with a list of the human forebears of Christ), and the eagle John (for his exalted contemplation of Christ). But this was certainly not in the mind of the author of Revelation. The Babylonians thought of the constellations as animals (the bull, the lion, the eagle, etc.). In Ezekiel's accommodation, these animals support the firmament or sky over which God sits on his throne, the stars being the eyes of the animals. John has, in turn, apparently accommodated this tradition to the Jewish tradition of the cherubim and seraphim, the angels who surround the divine throne and constantly sing God's praises.

The hymn they sing (4:8) echoes that which Isaiah heard the seraphim singing (Is 6:3). They omit "the whole earth is full of his glory," probably because John does not feel that the earth as he knows it fully reflects God's glory—it will ultimately disappear. But 4:9 appears to be in tension with this unceasing praise of God, since it indicates a periodic worship at which the twenty-four elders prostrate themselves (see also 5:8, 14; 11:16; 19:4). The problem is only apparent, however, for in any worship praise can be constant; yet periodically it swells to greater intensity. The elders' periodic worship is usually called forth by a crisis on earth, in which the important communion which the saints share with the earthly community is demonstrated.

Casting their crowns before the throne (4:10) reflects the practice known from the Roman world in which subject kings would cast their crowns before the emperor. One thinks of the sainted Queen Elizabeth of Hungary, who on entering the church would remove her crown. When asked why, she replied, "How can I wear my crown of gold in the house of my Lord who wears a crown of thorns?" Theologically, the meaning of this scene is that the saints, whether here on earth or in the glory of heaven, are a royal people, but they get that status from the Lord, and they must constantly proclaim its source.

The hymn of the elders (4:11) is a praise of God the Creator, in whose inscrutable free will lies the mystery of the very existence of everything.

INTRODUCING THE LAMB, VICTOR, AND REVEALER

[1]I saw a scroll in the right hand of the one who sat on the throne. It had writing on both sides and was sealed with seven seals. [2]Then I saw a mighty angel who proclaimed in a loud voice, "Who is worthy to open the scroll and break its seals?" [3]But no one in heaven or on earth or under the earth was able to open the scroll or to examine it. [4]I shed many tears because no one was found worthy to open the scroll or to examine it. One of the elders said to me, "Do not weep. The lion of the tribe of Judah, the root of David, has triumphed, enabling him to open the scroll with its seven seals."

[6]Then I saw standing in the midst of the throne and the four living creatures and the elders a Lamb that seemed to have been slain. He had seven horns and seven eyes; these are the [seven] spirits of God sent out into the whole world. [7]He came and received the scroll from the right hand of the one who sat on the throne. [8]When he took it, the four living creatures and the twenty-four elders fell down before the Lamb. Each of the elders held a harp and gold bowls filled with incense, which are the prayers of the holy ones. [9]They sang a new hymn:

"Worthy are you to receive the scroll
and to break open its seals,
for you were slain and with your
    blood you purchased for God

those from every tribe and tongue,
  people and nation.
[10]You made them a kingdom and priests for our God,
  and they will reign on earth."
  [11]I looked again and heard the voices of many angels
who surrounded the throne and the living creatures and
the elders. They were countless in number, [12]and they
cried out in a loud voice:
  "Worthy is the Lamb that was slain
to receive power and riches, wisdom
    and strength,
  honor and glory and blessing."
  [13]Then I heard every creature in heaven and on earth
and under the earth and in the sea, everything in the universe, cry out:
  "To the one who sits on the throne and
    to the Lamb
  be blessing and honor, glory and might,
    forever and ever."
  [14]The four living creatures answered, "Amen," and the
elders fell down and worshiped. **Revelation 5:1-14**

✧ ✧ ✧

Though the one on the throne cannot be seen, there is a
scroll in his right hand. It is written on both sides, indicating
the completeness of the revelation it contains. It is probably a
book-scroll, the leaves being bound together so that when
rolled up page-edges would be exposed. These bear seven
seals. As each seal is broken, something of the book will be
revealed, namely a glimpse of future events. The Lamb, of
course, won the right to open the seals long before the writing
of Revelation, so it is not impossible that some of the events
have already happened (for example, the death of the martyrs
referred to in the fifth seal). In general, however, opening the

seal not only reveals an event of the future but permits it to actually happen.

There is great drama and suspense here. The angel asks the question, "Who is worthy?" (5:2). The angels are not—and in this the Book of Revelation differs from the apocalyptic Book of Enoch, which can be read by the angels—though only by them. But neither is there any other creature who can open or read the scroll (5:3).

John the seer weeps—not because he is deprived of a knowledge of the future, but because the plan of God's triumphant justice (see Rom 1:17) cannot be released upon the world. His chosen ones, impoverished and persecuted, cry to him day and night (Lk 18:7), but there is no answer. Finally one of the elders (the heavenly counterpart of the earthly church) tells the seer that his tears of defeat will be turned to tears of joy. The right to open the scroll has been won by the *lion of the tribe of Judah* (5:5).

The triumphant prophecy of Jacob to his sons centuries earlier has now been fulfilled: "Judah, like a lion's whelp, you have grown up on prey, my son. He crouches like a lion recumbent, the king of beasts" (Gn 49:9). Combined with the prophecy of the *root of David*, the ideal royal Messiah whose kingdom would be one of perfect peace (Is 11:1-10), the image sums up the redemptive work of Christ in terms of victory (see 22:16).

With John, we have heard of a lion and expect to see one. Instead, between the throne of God and the elders appears a lamb (5:6)! The triumphant language of Genesis 49:9 had not prepared us for this. Although had we read closely the prophecy of the peaceable kingdom in Isaiah 11:6-7, we would have noticed that lamb and lion are at peace together. Another surprise: the lamb has been slain, and yet is standing! Thus in a single powerful paradox John provides an image which sums up the Servant-Messiah theology of the synoptic Gospels.

The Lion of Judah (the Messiah) is the Suffering Servant of Isaiah 52-53: "Like a lamb led to the slaughter or a sheep before the shearers" (Is 53:7). This in turn, echoes Jeremiah 11:19: "I, like a trusting lamb, was led to slaughter." The title *lamb* for Christ, of course, does not appear in the synoptic Gospels, only in the fourth Gospel. There it appears usually as *amnos,* probably referring to the lamb's innocence rather than to his imminent sacrifice (Jn 1:29). The word here is *arnios,* which in the fourth Gospel appears only once (Jn 21:15). However, it is the seer's favorite title for Christ, appearing in Revelation 29 times!

The standing lamb is the risen Christ, yet just as in John 20:24-29, he bears the marks of his sacrifice, now glorious. As with the standing Lamb, so will it be with his martyrs: they will bear forever the marks of their sacrifice, which are now marks of their victory.

There is an implicit lesson here as well, for those whose witness to Christ involves suffering of any kind. The hurts received, be they physical or emotional, are not erased when they are healed. Resurrection is not plastic surgery, nor is the healing of hurtful memories a spiritual lobotomy. As with the Lamb, the wounds are transformed by Christ's resurrection power to become badges of victory and windows of hope for others.

If we take the seven horns and eyes literally, the Lamb may look grotesque. But these are symbolic, the horns representing power (Nm 23:22; Dt 33:17; 1 Sm 2:1), and the eyes representing divine knowledge and wisdom (Zec 4:10). More specifically, they represent the seven spirits whom the Lamb now possesses to send out to the earth. Here again is the mixture of angelology and pneumatology typical of Revelation.

Notice that the elders give the Lamb the same worship they give to God (5:8; 4:10). The offering of incense was a special function of the Old Testament priests (1 Sm 2:28). Here the incense that rises (5:8) is the prayers of the saints (Ps 141:2). The saints on earth or the saints in heaven? Both meanings are possible here. In 6:10 the souls of the slain martyrs are under the heavenly altar, and they intercede.

Whenever new mercies of the Lord were experienced, it was common to "sing a new song to the Lord" (Ps 33:3; 40:4; 96:1; 97:1; 144:9; 149:1). In Isaiah 42:9 the Lord announces new events. These inspire a new song (Is 42:10). Here the new song proclaims the new world made possible by the Lamb's sacrifice (5:9).

The question of 5:2, "Who is worthy?" finds its answer here. Three reasons for the worthiness of the Lamb are given:

1. He was slain as the Paschal lamb (1 Cor 5:7; 1 Pt 1:18-19).

2. He has purchased a people by his blood. It is the Passover image of liberation here, like the ransom of prisoners of war.

3. He has made them a kingdom and priests (5:10). The new people of God are a priestly people (1 Pt 2:5,9), a fulfillment of the Old Testament covenant promise (Ex 19:6). But the emphasis falls on their kingly role—and they will reign not in heaven but *on earth.*

This is a very significant detail for the Book of Revelation. As Elizabeth Schüssler-Fiorenza has pointed out, John modifies the baptismal formula in 1:5-6 to give it a more sociopolitical twist. Christ continues his reign through Christians presently on earth. The church is the alternative to the Roman Empire! Is this a present realization? Or only a future realization (equivalent to the thousand-year reign in 20:4)? It is hard to be certain. Some Greek versions have the present "they reign," while others have the future "they will reign." In any case, it is crucial that Revelation does not consider the Christian life to end in a rejection of the world or an escape from it but, as in the Lord's prayer, in the coming of God's kingdom and the Lamb's here on earth.

After the countless heavenly hosts and the elders give glory to the Lamb (5:11-12), they are joined by every creature on earth and under the earth and in the sea as well (that symbol of the mysterious chaotic forces still to be tamed, 5:13). In the Old Testament, those in sheol (the abode of the dead) were understood to be incapable of praising God (Ps 6:6; 30:10; Is 38:18). But here they do, for the victorious Christ has burst the bonds of death (see 1 Pt 3:19). In 5:13-14, there is the climax of the entire section that began in Chapter 4 with the praise of God the Creator, then focused on the Lamb and his redemptive victory, giving him equal glory (Chapter 5). Now finally both are united in one cosmic praise: "to him who sits on the throne and to the Lamb." The cycle begun with the heavenly praise (5:8-12) was echoed by all of cosmic creation (5:13). Now it returns to heaven as the living creatures and the elders say, "Amen!" (5:14).

✧ ✧ ✧

Reflection

God, who is pure spirit, may be imaged in many ways. The restraint of John is admirable. He gives no physical traits of the "one seated upon the throne" other than to tell us that the scroll of revelation is in his right hand. The throne, like the person of God himself, is surrounded in luminous mystery. But one thing the scene tells us powerfully: God is King. The future is in his hand. Yet it will also be made by human choices, good ones and bad ones. Even so, it is only with God's permission that the successive stages of history unfold. These phases of history, however, are opened not by God but by the Lamb, to whom is given the Lordship of history. We on earth may be caught in the midst of one of the scenes of trial and chaos like those about to be revealed. We may wonder where are God and the Lamb. The vision of the heavenly throne and the Lamb reassures us that ultimately God is in control. In the end the Lamb, who cues each new phase of history, will conquer.

Questions

1. In the vision of the heavenly worship, what is meant by the rainbow? the sea? the twenty-four elders? the four living creatures and their song of praise? *Rainbow p. 98 Gn 9:12-17*
   Sea – Ezekiel 1:22-26 – Purification before entering presence all mighty – persecution, martyrdom
   24 elders – Heavenly council – 12 Tribes
   4 Living Creatures – angels, 99 12 disciples

2. What does this scene mean for us today?

3. Explain the Lamb who is worthy to open the scroll. *p. 101*
   Only Jesus's triumph. Lion of the tribe of Judah.

4. How does the standing yet pierced Lamb give meaning to *p. 103* our suffering today? *The Lamb has been slain but he is standing. An image of Servant – Messiah. Our hurts are not erased when healed but badges of victory*

5. Has God used the healing of my wounds to increase my compassion for others? Have my wounds become badges of victory?

Prayer

Heavenly Father, in faith I join all the heavenly host in proclaiming you King, Lord of heaven and earth. You have crowned me with goodness and kindness as your child, but I cast my crown before your throne to proclaim that all I am and have comes from you. And I adore the Lamb slain but standing, for he won back for me the crown I lost through sin. His victory is also my victory. He is indeed worthy to receive all blessing and honor and glory forever. Amen.

PART TWO

✧ ✧ ✧

The Drama Unfolds

FOUR

Opening the Seals
of Chaos and Suffering
(6:1–7:17)

H UNDREDS OF THOUSANDS DIE in African famine. War in Iraq and Kuwait is followed by widespread disease. A volcano asleep for six hundred years leaves Philippine cities in ashes. AIDS is reaching epidemic proportions. What is the Christian interpretation of these things and response to them? Do they mean the end is near? Will only 144,000 be saved? Does the church of the martyrs and the message of John have anything to tell us about all this? In short, is God speaking through cosmic disasters and persecutions? If so, what is he saying? John the seer is given insight into the mystery in what follows.

OPENING THE FIRST SIX SEALS

¹Then I watched while the Lamb broke open the first of the seven seals, and I heard one of the four living creatures cry out in a voice like thunder, "Come forward." ²I looked, and there was a white horse, and its rider had a

bow. He was given a crown, and he rode forth victorious to further his victories.

³When he broke open the second seal, I heard the second living creature cry out, "Come forward." ⁴Another horse came out, a red one. Its rider was given power to take peace away from the earth, so that people would slaughter one another. And he was given a huge sword.

⁵When he broke open the third seal, I heard the third living creature cry out, "Come forward." I looked, and there was a black horse, and its rider held a scale in his hand. ⁶I heard what seemed to be a voice in the midst of the four living creatures. It said, "A ration of wheat costs a day's pay, and three rations of barley cost a day's pay. But do not damage the olive oil or the wine."

⁷When he broke open the fourth seal, I heard the voice of the fourth living creature cry out, "Come forward." ⁸I looked, and there was a pale green horse. Its rider was named Death, and Hades accompanied him. They were given authority over a quarter of the earth, to kill with sword, famine, and plague, and by means of the beasts of the earth.

⁹When he broke open the fifth seal, I saw underneath the altar the souls of those who had been slaughtered because of the witness they bore to the word of God. ¹⁰They cried out in a loud voice, "How long will it be, holy and true master, before you sit in judgment and avenge our blood on the inhabitants of the earth?" ¹¹Each of them was given a white robe, and they were told to be patient a little while longer until the number was filled of their fellow servants and brothers who were going to be killed as they had been.

¹²Then I watched while he broke open the sixth seal, and there was a great earthquake; the sun turned as black as dark sackcloth and the whole moon became like blood. ¹³The stars in the sky fell to the earth like unripe figs shaken loose from the tree in a strong wind. ¹⁴Then the

sky was divided like a torn scroll curling up, and every mountain and island was moved from its place. ¹⁵The kings of the earth, the nobles, the military officers, the rich, the powerful, and every slave and free person hid themselves in caves and among mountain crags. ¹⁶They cried out to the mountains and the rocks, "Fall on us and hide us from the face of the one who sits on the throne and from the wrath of the Lamb, ¹⁷because the great day of their wrath has come and who can withstand it?"

Revelation 6:1-17

From here to the end of the book, we have five cycles of visions. Each cycle follows a threefold pattern of suffering or persecution of the church, punishment or judgment of the nations, ending in the triumph of God, the Lamb, and his followers (or some other image of salvation). It is not clear whether the author intends to describe specific historical events or is using traditional apocalyptic language to portray the future in general terms. The similarity of the events in the seals with the synoptic apocalypses is striking.

The first five seals describe war, international strife, famine, pestilence (death and Hades), and persecutions. The sixth seal reveals earthquakes, eclipse of the sun and bloodying of the moon, falling stars, people calling on the rocks to fall on them, shaking the powers of heaven, and four destroying winds. All of these are found in one form or another in Mark 13:7-9, 24-25; Matthew 24:6-7, 9, 29; and Luke 21:9-12, 25-26.

Moreover, the seer has adapted Zechariah's visions of the four horsemen (Zec 1:8-11) and the four chariots (Zec 6:1-8) to his purpose. These similarities would argue for seeing the events as a *general* interpretation of the future. It seems unlikely, in any case, that John is giving us a chronological sequence.

Moreover, if he is living in the last decade of the first century, he has already experienced or learned of some of these events in his lifetime, as we know from Roman history.

1. There were widespread earthquakes in A.D. 60, one of which destroyed Laodicea.

2. The Parthians handed the Roman armies a humiliating defeat in the east in A.D. 62.

3. Fire destroyed much of Rome in A.D. 64, and the Christians were blamed and persecuted for it.

4. Nero's suicide in A.D. 68 precipitated political chaos as four claimants fought for the throne.

5. The Jewish-Roman war lasted four years, ending with the destruction of Jerusalem and the temple in A.D. 70.

6. Vesuvius erupted in A.D. 79, wiping out the cities of Pompeii and Herculaneum and covering the earth with a cloud of darkness that made people fear the end of the world.

7. In A.D. 92 there was a serious famine because of the failure of grain crops.

It is likely, then, that the author is selecting events typical of chaos and suffering, and projecting them on the screen of the future with an intent similar to the apocalyptic discourses in the synoptic Gospels. These awesome events are foretold not to frighten the disciples but to reassure them. These are signs of the final consummation of all things, but the end is not yet (Mk 13:7). Hence, Christians should not expect to be spared some of these world calamities but to persevere in their faith. Here the author wants to show that the Lamb knows all these events. It is only with his permission that they take place. The historical process must unfold, so that his ultimate triumph and that of his followers may be consummated on earth.

Generals who were victorious in war usually rode a white horse in their victory parade. But in the first seal (6:2) the meaning of the rider on the white horse (6:2) is disputed. Some scholars, noting the similarity with the rider of the white horse in 19:11-16, have proposed that here the scene represents the victorious gospel. But there the rider is armed with a sword, a symbol of the Word of God (Wis 18:16; Heb 4:12; Eph 6:17). Here the *bow* suggests the only mounted archers known at the time, the Parthians, who had defeated the Roman armies on the eastern frontier in A.D. 62. Since John also expects an invasion from the east (9:14; 16:12), he is probably using the past event to project and predict the coming of a power that will defeat Rome.

The second seal (6:3) symbolizes bloodshed and international strife and warfare (the sword). The third seal (6:5-6) portrays famine. Barley was the food of the poor (2 Kgs 7:1, 16, 18); it was three times cheaper than wheat and was also used to feed animals (1 Kgs 5:8). In ordinary times one day's pay, the Roman denarius, would buy about ten times more than that indicated here, so that the breadwinner could buy a liter of grain (considered the daily ration at the time) and still have sufficient left over to care for other needs of the family. But here that single basic need takes the entire wage. Wine and oil, superfluities by contrast to bread, will be in abundance (as they were in the famine of A.D. 92).

The sickly green or pale yellow horse of the fourth seal (6:7-8) is the color of pestilence or death. This horse has two riders, the second being the netherworld (the abode of the dead). Although the sword and famine also came with the second and third horses, here the new elements are plague and wild beasts. John is echoing Ezekiel 14:21, where the same four elements appear: "I send Jerusalem my four cruel punishments, the sword, famine, wild beasts and pestilence," suggesting again that traditional imagery has been projected into a general description of the future.

But the traditional imagery is less evident in the fifth seal (6:9-11). Although the martyrs were slain on earth, God received their death as a sacrifice on his heavenly altar from which, very realistically, their blood ran down. As Jews considered life to be in the blood, the souls of the martyrs thus are preserved under the altar. The Greek literally reads, "They were slaughtered for God's Word and for holding to the testimony," that is, the testimony of Jesus himself whose sacrifice they join and continue.

In Jewish thought, the blood of the innocent cried to heaven for vengeance (Gn 4:10). Thus some of the woes to come are seen as visited upon the world because of its shedding of innocent blood. If the cries of the just on earth win a hearing from God (18:7; Sir 32:15-22), the shed blood of the martyrs gives the blessed special intercessory power. They beg for God's justice to be revealed, for he is the "holy and true master."

The Christian is forbidden to seek revenge (Rom 12:19). But certainly he should pray that injustices be righted, whether by the conversion of the sinner or vindication of the oppressed. In passing it should be noted that this text clearly assumes that the saints in heaven intercede for the church on earth. The cries of intercession do not mean that they are unhappy, for they are given a white robe to wear, a symbol of immortality (6:11). They are told that the full plan of God is not yet fulfilled, for more martyrs are to follow. In this John is telling his readers that they too must be ready for the ultimate sacrifice, should it be asked of them.

The events of the sixth seal (6:12-17) are given the most extensive description. Yet here, too, traditional imagery is used to predict future events. The drama is cosmic, but even an examination of the text indicates that we should be careful not to identify each detail as a literal prophecy. After the stars fall, the sky is rolled up and every mountain and island is moved. Yet the inhabitants of the earth hide in the caves and rocks of the earth, imploring the mountains to fall on them (6:15-16). Consequently, as was so often the case in the Old Testament, cosmic imagery is probably being used here to describe a political event on earth that is "earthshaking."

Isaiah 2:10-21 provides an excellent background for our text. The prophet, who had experienced a great earthquake in his youth (Am 1:2; Zec 14:5), describes the coming "Day of the Lord," which was fulfilled in the Assyrian invasion, when people were seeking refuge in caves and rocks "from the terror of the Lord ... when he arises to overawe the earth." Falling stars, darkened sun and moon are used in Isaiah 13:10 to describe the fall of Babylon. Similar images are used to describe the death of Pharaoh in Ezekiel 32:7-8 and a plague of locusts in Joel 2:10.

John the seer does not identify the political event he is predicting. Based on the similarity with Isaiah 2:10-21, it would be the collapse of a proud and oppressive earthly system and that, in the experience of the author, would have been the Roman Empire.

People of every rank prefer to be crushed by the mountains and rocks rather than face the *wrath of God and the Lamb* (6:16). Though the wrath of God is frequently mentioned in Revelation (11:18; 14:10, 19; 15:7; 16:1, 19; 19:15), the Lamb is always depicted as gentle and peaceful. How do we explain this paradoxical description here?

First of all, when closely analyzed, the wrath of God is not God "losing his temper" in an arbitrary decision to punish. In reality it is nothing else than the effect which human beings experience when they choose to turn from God (see Rom 1:18-32; Is 9:18; Ps 38:2-6). One cannot turn from the light without experiencing darkness, nor from love without experiencing bitterness, nor from life without experiencing death (Is 24:4-6).

As for the Lamb, he won his victory by the cross. His very meekness provoked an even more violent reaction on the part of those who could not understand God's way of overcoming evil. Their violence would have been more "justified" in their own eyes, if Jesus had reacted with violence.

Notice here that "the wrath of God and the Lamb" is placed on the lips of those who are *enemies* of God and the Lamb. As Caird remarks, it is the supreme conquest of Satan to persuade men and women that the God of love is the source of wrath. Faced with the love and forgiveness of the sacrificed Lamb, they see only a figure of vengeance: "The wicked man flees although no one pursues him" (Prv 28:1). The mention of the Lamb is important at the conclusion of this chapter, because it was at his action that the scroll of revelation was opened. The Lamb dominates the whole scene—at the beginning as revealer, at the end as judge.

The inhabitants of the earth think that the day of God's punishment has come (6:17). This is not John's view, for the role of the martyrs has not yet been fully played out. Worse woes still await the unbelieving world.

What might all of this mean for us today? Cosmic disasters, wars, and other forms of violence are invitations to the ungodly to turn to God the Creator and Redeemer, the author of peace and order, the ultimate source of all stability and wholeness. Bloodshed and violence, the effects of sin, proclaim the need for salvation. For those sealed with the blood of Christ, such events (whose effects they also often suffer) are an invitation to enter into the redemptive suffering of Jesus, continued now in the church. Christians are rarely spared the sufferings that befall the world. The atom bomb dropped on Nagasaki hit not the palace of the warlords but the densest Catholic population of Japan. In trying to make sense of this tragedy, some of the Catholic survivors said that perhaps in God's strange, permissive will it happened thus because the Christians were more ready than their nonbelieving countrymen to meet God—a merciful choice which they might offer in redeeming love for the conversion of their country.

A PAUSE: THE SEALING OF THOUSANDS

¹After this I saw four angels standing at the four corners of the earth, holding back the four winds of the earth so that no wind could blow on land or sea or against any tree. ²Then I saw another angel come up from the East, holding the seal of the living God. He cried out in a loud voice to the four angels who were given power to damage the land and the sea, ³"Do not damage the land or the sea or the trees until we put the seal on the foreheads of the servants of our God." ⁴I heard the number of those who had been marked with the seal, one hundred and forty-four thousand marked from every tribe of the Israelites: ⁵twelve thousand were marked from the tribe of Judah, twelve thousand from the tribe of Reuben, ⁶twelve thousand from the tribe of Gad, twelve thousand from the tribe of Asher, twelve thousand from the tribe of Naphtali, twelve thousand from the tribe of Manasseh, ⁷twelve thousand from the tribe of Simeon, twelve thousand from the tribe of Levi, twelve thousand from the tribe of Issachar, ⁸twelve thousand from the tribe of Zebulun, twelve thousand from the tribe of Joseph, and twelve thousand were marked from the tribe of Benjamin.

Revelation 7:1-8

At this point we expect the opening of the seventh seal, but our suspense is further heightened by a dramatic pause. The faithful are sealed, so as to stand unharmed by what is to be unleashed next. The fact that they were not sealed before the woes of the first six seals is theologically significant: Christians are not to be spared the tribulations which the entire earth will experience. They will only be preserved from the demonic powers that would lead them to apostasy.

In this John differs radically from his Jewish contemporary

who wrote the Psalms of Solomon. According to the latter (15:6-10), the righteous will be spared all the evils which the wicked suffer in the last days, such as famine, sword, and pestilence. A similar view is held by those Christians who hold that there will be a rapture which will spare faithful Christians from the tribulation of the final times. But this is clearly not the view of John.

The faithful will suffer with the rest of the world. Many will endure martyrdom as well (see also 13:7). For this they will be sealed, not to immunize them or give them escape from suffering, but to empower them with fidelity. This strengthening for the final testing is the answer to the last petition of the Lord's prayer: "Lead us not into temptation" really means, "Do not let us succumb in the trial."

In Zechariah 6:5 the four winds are equivalent to the four horses. In 7:1, however, they probably represent a destructive, even demonic power that must be restrained in favor of the elect (compare the "restrainer" in 2 Thes 2:6-7). The great calm heightens the suspense before the storm but also provides the chance for sealing the elect.

What is this "seal of God" mentioned in 7:3? John again borrows from Ezekiel 9:1-7, giving it a new twist. Is it the seal of baptism (2 Cor 1:22)? Who are the servants? And who are the 144,000?

The number is clearly symbolic: the square of twelve, and thousands meaning tribes. If John calls them the tribes of Israel, he could hardly have meant the old Israel. Christians now thought of themselves as the new Israel of God (Gal 6:16; Jas 1:1), seeing in the twelve apostles the symbolic fulfillment of the twelve tribes (Mt 19:28; Lk 22:30).

Did he mean only the Jewish Christians? That would be very strange; in that case only they, and not the gentile Christians, would need the seal in order to endure the trial and enter the presence of God. Thus the best solution is simply that John is using a Jewish collective category (as he so often does) to describe both Jewish and gentile members. But does he mean the entire church or only the martyrs? The crowd that is sealed in 7:3-8 *before* the tribulation is the same crowd portrayed in their anticipated glory *after* the tribulation (7:9-17). Since these clearly are the victorious martyrs (7:14), the seal must be something more than the seal of baptism. It is the special grace of perseverance and protection given to those called to martyrdom. The fact that they are so numerous means that John is expecting thousands of his fellow Christians to give their lives in the coming persecution.

ANOTHER PAUSE: THE VICTORY SONG OF THE MARTYRS

[9]After this I had a vision of a great multitude, which no one could count, from every nation, race, people, and tongue. They stood before the throne and before the Lamb, wearing white robes and holding palm branches in their hands. [10]They cried out in a loud voice:

"Salvation comes from our God, who
        is seated on the throne,
    and from the Lamb."

[11]All the angels stood around the throne and around the elders and the four living creatures. They prostrated themselves before the throne, worshiped God, [12]and exclaimed:

"Amen. Blessing and glory, wisdom
        and thanksgiving,
    honor, power, and might
    be to our God forever and ever.
        Amen."

[13]Then one of the elders spoke up and said to me, "Who are these wearing white robes, and where did they come from?" [14]I said to him, "My lord, you are the one who knows." He said to me, "These are the ones who have survived the time of great distress; they have washed

their robes and made them white in the blood of the
Lamb.

[15]"For this reason they stand before God's throne
and worship him day and night in his temple.
The one who sits on the throne will shelter them.
[16] They will not hunger or thirst anymore,
nor will the sun or any heat strike them.
[17]For the Lamb who is in the center of the throne
will shepherd them
and lead them to springs of life-giving water,
and God will wipe away every tear from their eyes."

Revelation 7:9-17

❖ ❖ ❖

The sequence of scenes now leaves the chronological order.
With John, we have an anticipation of the glory the martyrs
will receive in heaven *after* they have passed through the great
tribulation. In this scene it is not all the blessed but specifically
the martyrs that are envisioned (7:14).

It is true that a heavenly reward awaits all those who are
faithful, even if they are not martyred (as we saw in 2:10). The
image of washing one's robes in the blood of the Lamb might
later be applied to water baptism. But there is no doubt that
John is thinking of the "baptism of blood" about to be visited
upon Christians throughout the empire. So the "great crowd"
of 7:9 is the same as the 144,000 of 7:4-8. What was described
there in terms of the tribes of Israel is described here on a
cosmic scale.

It was passages such as these that led Christians, even after
the end of the Roman persecution, to hold martyrdom in such
high regard that Augustine would have to reassure his flock
that they could still attain eternal life without it (see commentary on 2:10 above).

White robes signify here (7:9) as elsewhere immortality,
even resurrected bodily glory. Palm branches were symbols of

victory and joy after war (1 Mc 13:51; 2 Mc 10:7; Jn 12:13). The word "salvation" in 7:10, though capable of extension to all the elect, means the grace of salvation for the martyr. Probably no one better than the martyr himself or herself realizes that martyrdom is a grace rather than a work—a gift received from the Lord rather than something one sets out to do. It is only when every other path is closed that the call to martyrdom becomes clear. In T.S. Eliot's *Murder in the Cathedral,* St. Thomas Becket realizes this when, after brushing aside other lesser temptations, he is tempted to seek martyrdom for his own glory. Recognizing this, Thomas responds: "The last temptation is the greatest treason, to do the right deed for the wrong reason."

In 7:14, the Greek participle translated "have survived" is in the present tense "are coming through," so that John actually sees the martyrs still processing in. The "great distress" is not the final closure of time but the massive persecution about to break out. Martyrdom is a grace, but it is also one in which the martyrs have chosen to cooperate by making use of the blood of the Lamb ("they have washed... "). In the martyrdom of Jesus they have found the power to win the victory.

Hymns or hymn fragments, possibly used already in the Christian communities known to John, appear in 7:15-17, as they did in 7:10 and 7:12. The martyrs are a priestly people, sheltered by the divine Shekinah, the cloud of glory (7:15). Fulfilling the prophecy of Isaiah 49:10, all their hungers and thirsts are satisfied, for God himself is the fountain of life (Ps 36:10; Jn 4:14; 7:37-39). Suffering will be no more (7:16).

The Lamb becomes the shepherd! In this single image the seer incorporates the Old Testament description of the Lord as shepherd (Ps 23) and the New Testament fulfillment in Jesus, the good shepherd (Jn 10:11, 14; Heb 13:20; 1 Pt 2:25). Again, as Isaiah prophesied (25:8), every tear will be wiped from their eyes.

❖ ❖ ❖

Reflection

Christians like ourselves may not be called to martyrdom. Yet in the midst of troubles, great or small, we need to be sealed with God's protection lest the evils we go through infect our spirit and we, who are supposed to be part of the solution to evil in the world, become part of the problem instead. Such is the prayer we pray, "Lead us not into temptation, but deliver us in our struggle with evil."

Questions

1. Were any of the descriptions of the seals familiar to the people in John's day? *p. 113 - 114*

2. What happens when we turn from God? *p. 117*
One cannot turn from legal - ehp. darkness From love to bitterness From life to death.

3. Why are the followers of Christ sealed?
They are not spared Tribulations but will be preserved from demonic powers that lead to apostasy. p. 119

4. Who receives the seal? Who shepherds those who are sealed?
13:7 Christians, the faithful To empower c fidelity.

5. How does this apply to the church today? To my life? *p. 118*
Inviting the ungodly to turn to God. To enter into the redemption suffering of Jesus

Prayer

Lord, equip me with your armor—the shield of faith, the helmet of salvation, and the sword of the Spirit, your Word—so that I may not be overcome by the trials of my life but stand firm under your protection and in doing good never grow tired. Seal me too with the seal of your Holy Spirit, that I may ever be faithful to you, even should you call me to martyrdom. Amen.

FIVE

Sounding the Trumpets
(8:1–10:11)

C OSMIC DISASTERS have visited the earth before. Were the dinosaurs wiped out by a passing comet or collision with a star? Will things like this happen again? Is the depletion of the ozone layer spelling doom for humanity? Will the destruction of the rain forests choke the rest of the earth? Will a nuclear holocaust wipe out nations? Will our water and air become poisoned by overindustrialization? These are questions that bother every thinking person on earth today. Does the Book of Revelation have anything to say about them? What are we to make of the frightening images of cosmic destruction that John is now going to show us? And if these disasters are punishments visited upon God's good earth, how are we to square this with our conception of a God of love?

These may not be the questions John had in mind. We see in this section the great importance of prayer and intercession in relation to these "chastisements." In any case, we approach the text with our modern questions and anxieties. Before jumping to conclusions, let us accompany John through his visions and try to hear his message on his own terms.

OPENING THE SEVENTH SEAL

¹When he broke open the seventh seal, there was silence in heaven for about half an hour. ²And I saw that the seven angels who stood before God were given seven trumpets.

³Another angel came and stood at the altar, holding a gold censer. He was given a great quantity of incense to offer, along with the prayers of all the holy ones, on the gold altar that was before the throne. ⁴The smoke of the incense along with the prayers of the holy ones went up before God from the hand of the angel. ⁵Then the angel took the censer, filled it with burning coals from the altar, and hurled it down to the earth. There were peals of thunder, rumblings, flashes of lightning, and an earthquake.   **Revelation 8:1-5**

✧ ✧ ✧

The seventh seal is the last, so we expect the end of God's plan. But the end does not come. Instead we have another interlude of heavenly liturgy, then a new series of visions introduced by the seven trumpets. This in turn introduces the unnumbered visions of Chapters 12-14, then seven bowls of plagues, then the fall of Babylon and the last battle.

The theory of R.H. Charles, that John is depicting a strict chronology of events, has been largely discarded for it runs into insurmountable difficulties. Likewise the theory that Revelation is structured on a pattern of weeks, for this too runs into the problem of chronological sequence. Besides, John quits counting when he describes unnumbered visions. Caird's view is that the numbered visions are general views of the totality of divine judgment. The unnumbered visions are close-up, detailed studies.

The view that has gained greater acceptance is that the series of interlocking visions (for example, the seventh seal opening up another series of seven) is a literary device. It enables the author to describe the same reality from different points of view. Thus, just as the seven letters address the churches, the seven seals deal largely with the people of the earth, the seven trumpets present the same reality from a cosmic viewpoint, and the seven bowls describe the events in terms of the Old Testament plagues (though John also uses the plague images earlier as well). The numbered visions deal with historical events largely in traditional terms, that is, using stock images of the Old Testament or the Jewish apocalypses. The unnumbered visions, however, while using much traditional imagery, are more revealing of John's particular theology. We will see all of this in detail as the book unfolds.

The silence in 8:1 is not only a dramatic pause, heightening the suspense—it has a theological purpose. A Jewish tradition recorded in the Talmud states that the angels in heaven sing throughout the night, then cease during the daytime in order for Israel's praises to be heard. But here the heavenly choirs praise God day and night (4:8-9). That praise is now interrupted in order to allow the prayers of God's people on earth to be heard. This is also the meaning of the introduction of the angels with the trumpets in 8:2. They are introduced but they cannot blow the trumpets until the prayers of the saints have their effect (8:3-4).

The Old Testament altar of incense was made of gold (Nm 4:11). Incense was a symbol of prayer ascending to God (Ps 141:2). The prayers of the saints release the power of God to act in human history. It is not just the sacrifice of the martyrs here but the prayers of the whole church that are effective in God's plan. Therefore, if we are not called to martyrdom, we can at least participate in the intercessory power of the martyrs, by praying for the coming of the kingdom.

The Christian schooled in the meekness advocated in the Sermon on the Mount may find it difficult to handle what appears to be violence in the angel's hurling the censer to the earth (8:5)—to say nothing of the maiming of the earth and sky following the various trumpets. Can Revelation, which has come out of a movement founded by the gentle Jesus, be recommending the kind of prayer for vengeance that we find at times in the Old Testament (cf. Jer 15:15; 17:18)? Even there, however, Proverbs taught: "Rejoice not when your enemy falls, and when he stumbles, let not your heart exult, lest the Lord see it, be displeased with you, and withdraw his wrath from your enemy" (Prv 24:17).

Notice how in this passage, when men and women take vengeance into their own hands, they are likely to be interfering with God's way of dealing with the injustice. Or again: "If your enemy be hungry, give him food to eat, if he is thirsty, give him to drink; for live coals you will heap on his head, and the Lord will vindicate you" (Prv 25:21-22). Paul quotes this passage in Romans 12:20, adding: "Do not look for revenge but leave room for the wrath." The wrath of which Paul speaks here is God's wrath. For the wrath of humans does not accomplish the justice of God (Jas 1:20). God's wrath is not spite. It is his second-best gift to the one who has refused the first gift of his love; it is also given to bring humanity to repentance (Rom 2:4-11).

It is often a biblical way of speaking of the disintegrating consequences of humanity's evil choices (cf. Rom 1:18-32; cf. Is 9:17-19), like the hunger of the prodigal son which leads him to realize how much better it was in his father's house (Lk 15:16-17). Consequently, there can be no vengeance in the heart of the Christian who prays. But God does consider the prayer of the faithful, nonviolent Christian as a stimulus to his action in history.

SOUNDING THE FIRST FOUR TRUMPETS

[6]The seven angels who were holding the seven trumpets prepared to blow them.

⁷When the first one blew his trumpet, there came hail and fire mixed with blood, which was hurled down to the earth. A third of the land was burned up, along with a third of the trees and all green grass.

⁸When the second angel blew his trumpet, something like a large burning mountain was hurled into the sea. A third of the sea turned to blood, ⁹a third of the creatures living in the sea died, and a third of the ships were wrecked.

¹⁰When the third angel blew his trumpet, a large star burning like a torch fell from the sky. It fell on a third of the rivers and on the springs of water. ¹¹The star was called "Wormwood," and a third of all the water turned to wormwood. Many people died from this water, because it was made bitter.

¹²When the fourth angel blew his trumpet, a third of the sun, a third of the moon, and a third of the stars were struck, so that a third of them became dark. The day lost its light for a third of the time, as did the night.

¹³Then I looked again and heard an eagle flying high overhead cry out in a loud voice, "Woe! Woe! Woe to the inhabitants of the earth from the rest of the trumpet blasts that the three angels are about to blow!"

Revelation 8:6-13

The first four trumpets introduce natural disasters that touch earth, salt water, fresh water, and sky. In each case only a third of creation is touched, indicating that these disasters are not God's final judgment but an invitation to repentance.

The first woe (8:7) is a rerun of the seventh plague of Egypt: the hail (Ex 9:23-24), to which is added the blood and fire image from Joel 3:3. Here all the grass is destroyed. Yet in 9:4 the locusts are told not to harm the grass, a further indication that what we have here is not a chronological sequence. Rather the same mystery is being dramatized in a different way. The first plague upon Egypt turned the Nile into blood (Ex 7:14-24). This is the background for the second and third woes (8:8-11).

John's addition of the burning mountain has been explained by some as a fallen star—on the basis of Enoch's vision of "seven stars like great burning mountains" which turn out to be fallen angels (1 Enoch 18:13). In the Sibylline Oracles (5:158), a star falling into the sea brings about the destruction of Babylon, that is, Rome. But since a falling star brings about the third woe, it seems that the second woe is inspired by Jeremiah's prophecy against ancient Babylon: "I am coming against you, destroying mountain, destroyer of the entire earth," says the Lord; "I will stretch forth my hand against you, roll you down over the cliffs, and make you a burnt mountain" (Jer 51:25). Thus the mountain here is the Babylon of John's day (Rome) whose downfall, though certain, will bring much bloodshed upon the earth.

As the salty seas were polluted by the burning mountain, so the fresh waters are polluted by a falling star named Wormwood (8:10-11), a bitter plant used already in Jeremiah 9:14 and 23:15 as the Lord's punishment of the ungodly.

Behind the reference to the falling star is an ancient myth of Babylonian or Phoenician origin, explaining the natural phenomenon of the vanishing of the morning star at the rising of the sun. Heylel (Morning Star), a lesser god, tried to climb to the heavens to make himself king of the gods, but was driven from the sky by the rising sun.

Ezekiel used these mythical elements in his poetic funeral dirge for the king of ancient Babylon: "How you have fallen from the heavens, O morning star, son of the dawn! How are you cut down to the ground, you who mowed down the nations! You said in your heart, 'I will scale the heavens; above the stars of God I will set my throne; I will take my seat on the Mount of Assembly, in the recesses of the North [the mythical city of the gods]. I will ascend above the tops of the clouds; I will be like the Most High!' Yet down to the netherworld you go to the recesses of the pit" (Is 14:12-15). Jews listening to the reading of John's description here could easily make the connection with Rome and its tyrannical emperor.

The fourth woe (8:12) corresponds to the ninth plague, that of darkness, in Exodus 10:21-23, except that here the darkness is not total, for reasons mentioned above. An eagle or vulture (8:13) interrupts to alert us to more disastrous woes yet to come, this time on the inhabitants of the earth who, as the sequence will indicate, are unbelievers. If translated "eagle," the word may recall that the Lord brought Israel through the first Exodus "on eagle wings" (Ex 19:4). If translated "vulture," the image is one of doom: "Set a trumpet to your lips, for a vulture is over the house of the Lord, because they have broken my covenant, and transgressed my law" (Hos 8:1, *RSV*).

Again, it is helpful to recall that neither God in his providence nor Christians in their prayers are violent or destructive. The sins of the inhabitants of the earth have filled the cosmos with a toxic element that will eventually rain back upon them. Christians under persecution praying, "Thy kingdom come," simply ask that God, who continues to restrain the deadly effects in the hope of wider conversions, will move his plan ahead. Therefore, he releases partial disasters as warnings to convert before men's and women's self-made disaster overtakes them.

SOUNDING THE FIFTH TRUMPET

¹Then the fifth angel blew his trumpet, and I saw a star that had fallen from the sky to the earth. It was given the key for the passage to the abyss. ²It opened the passage to the abyss, and smoke came up out of the passage like smoke from a huge furnace. The sun and the air

were darkened by the smoke from the passage. ³Locusts came out of the smoke onto the land, and they were given the same power as scorpions of the earth. ⁴They were told not to harm the grass of the earth or any plant or any tree, but only those people who did not have the seal of God on their foreheads. ⁵They were not allowed to kill them but only to torment them for five months; the torment they inflicted was like that of a scorpion when it stings a person. ⁶During that time these people will seek death but will not find it, and they will long to die but death will escape them.

⁷The appearance of the locusts was like that of horses ready for battle. In their heads they wore what looked like crowns of gold; their faces were like human faces, ⁸and they had hair like women's hair. Their teeth were like lions' teeth, ⁹and they had chests like iron breastplates. The sound of their wings was like the sound of many horse-drawn chariots racing into battle. ¹⁰They had tails like scorpions, with stingers; with their tails they had power to harm people for five months. ¹¹They had as their king the angel of the abyss, whose name in Hebrew is Abaddon and in Greek Apollyon.

¹²The first woe has passed, but there are two more to come.   **Revelation 9:1-12**

❖ ❖ ❖

Though above in the third woe the star represented the fallen power of Rome, here it is a code name for an angel. The abyss (9:1) is the dark, formless chaos which the Lord at creation conquered by his Word (Gn 1:2-8), putting half up as the sky and the other half down as the waters of the earth. From ancient times it was a symbol of the dark side of creation which had become reinforced or released by the sins of the race. It was also the abode of the serpent (Am 9:3) or Leviathan, the mythical sea monster (Jb 3:8). God's creative act limited darkness and the watery abyss by driving them into the order of night and the seas. Both retain some warning for human beings that chaos and destruction lurk for those who reject the God of creative order.

By New Testament times the abyss was identified with *sheol,* the huge cavernous netherworld of fire where the fallen angels were kept for one thousand years (20:7-10). The shaft joining earth and the netherworld was kept locked, but here the key is given to the fallen star. However, the agents of the netherworld are not wholly independent of God. The key is *given* to them, and their action on earth is limited.

Much of the imagery here (9:2-11) is borrowed from Joel's dramatic description of the locust plague (Jl 1-2). Locusts coming over the horizon could well resemble a cloud of smoke darkening the sky (Jl 2:10). If they are enlarged grasshoppers, their heads would resemble those of horses (9:7), their antennae would resemble human hair, their ravenous teeth would be like those of lions (9:8), their faces would appear human, and their heads would be crowned by what *looked like* gold (9:7). Notice the emphasis on appearance. They can seduce, and they sting with their tails, from behind, suggesting deceptiveness.

It is obvious that these locusts are more than Joel's simple plague. They are demonic. Instead of injuring grass and plants, as ordinary locusts do, they injure people. The locusts of nature "have no king" (Prv 30:27), but these have one: the angel of the abyss (whose name in Aramaic and Greek means "destroyer," see 9:11). They work through human instruments, for they have human faces. Still their destructive power is limited. They do not touch those sealed by God (9:4); and even the unsealed are not killed but only stung for five months, the approximate lifetime of locusts.

SOUNDING THE SIXTH TRUMPET

[13]Then the sixth angel blew his trumpet, and I heard a voice coming from the [four] horns of the gold altar before God, [14]telling the sixth angel who held the trumpet, "Release the four angels who are bound at the banks of the great river Euphrates." [15]So the four angels were released, who were prepared for this hour, day, month, and year to kill a third of the human race. [16]The number of cavalry troops was two hundred million; I heard their number. [17]Now in my vision this is how I saw the horses and their riders. They wore red, blue, and yellow breastplates, and the horses' heads were like heads of lions, and out of their mouths came fire, smoke, and sulfur. [18]By these three plagues of fire, smoke, and sulfur that came out of their mouths a third of the human race was killed. [19]For the power of the horses is in their mouths and in their tails; for their tails are like snakes, with heads that inflict harm.

[20]The rest of the human race, who were not killed by these plagues, did not repent of the works of their hands, to give up the worship of demons and idols made from gold, silver, bronze, stone, and wood, which cannot see or hear or walk. [21]Nor did they repent of their murders, their magic potions, their unchastity, or their robberies.

Revelation 9:13-21

❖ ❖ ❖

The voice from the altar indicates that what is about to happen is a further answer to the prayers of the martyrs and the faithful (9:3-4). But how can so dreadful a plague possibly be willed either by God or by Christians? The author obviously means this question to be asked. Though he does not answer it here, it is clear that the plague, far from being God's primary intention, is rather the effect of human perversity. God withholds the chaotic fruits of humanity's sins for awhile (the destructive angels are bound) in hopes for repentance (see 9:20-21). But when this does not occur, he releases them (9:14-15) as a further call for repentance (9:20-21).

The dramatic elements of this scene are drawn from the memories of the Parthian Empire that lay beyond the Euphrates (9:14). It had defeated the Roman armies in 53 B.C. and again in A.D. 62. They were horsemen and archers. But the incredible numbers (two hundred million) and the apocalyptic description of the horses (heads of lions, tails of serpents) indicate that this is more than a political enemy (Hal Lindsey says it is Communist China!).

It is a demonic horde. The colors of their breastplates correspond to the plagues they unleash: fire (red), smoke (blue), and sulfur (yellow). Only a third of the race is killed (9:18) indicating that their work is still limited, in hopes that the rest will repent. The sins begin with idolatry (9:20), but others follow in its wake (9:21, as in Rom 1:18-32).

Perhaps a reflection on the function of dreams can help us understand what John is trying to do here. Dreams are often a projection of unconscious fears. Our imagination constructs a play. Unrestrained by conscious reasoning, it often projects our fears to apocalyptic proportions such as we see here. Our imagination often uses elements of previous experience and expands them to the cosmic. Some of the things we envision may actually come to pass. Others may simply be symbolic warnings of what the future holds unless we change our course of action (recall Scrooge's dreams in Charles Dickens' *A Christmas Carol*).

Even reason can sometimes project a horrible scenario of what could actually happen: for example, the fifty-three second televised animation I once saw of the nuclear destruction of Omaha. The function of the frightful scenario (in Revelation) has two purposes:

1. a call to repentance;
2. an assurance to those who do repent and to the faithful, that they will survive and conquer because of the Lamb.

In the context of bloody persecution, it is likely that there would be little hope that the preaching of the gospel would gradually chip away the evil, demonic powers of this world. Instead, there is a hardening of the forces until one final cosmic battle. This is not the only view of the role of the gospel in the world (Jesus spoke of it as a seed or leaven). Under the tyrant's sword, the image of gradualness gives way to a black-and-white issue of faith or disbelief.

A DIVERSION: THE LITTLE SCROLL

[1]Then I saw another mighty angel come down from heaven wrapped in a cloud, with a halo around his head; his face was like the sun and his feet were like pillars of fire. [2]In his hand he held a small scroll that had been opened. He placed his right foot on the sea and his left foot on the land, [3]and then he cried out in a loud voice as a lion roars. When he cried out, the seven thunders raised their voices, too. [4]When the seven thunders had spoken, I was about to write it down; but I heard a voice from heaven say, "Seal up what the seven thunders have spoken, but do not write it down." [5]Then the angel I saw standing on the sea and on the land raised his right hand to heaven [6]and swore by the one who lives forever and ever, who created heaven and earth and sea and all that is in them, "There shall be no more delay. [7]At the time when you hear the seventh angel blow his trumpet, the mysterious plan of God shall be fulfilled, as he promised to his servants the prophets."

[8]Then the voice that I had heard from heaven spoke

to me again and said, "Go, take the scroll that lies open in the hand of the angel who is standing on the sea and on the land." [9]So I went up to the angel and told him to give me the small scroll. He said to me, "Take and swallow it. It will turn your stomach sour, but in your mouth it will taste as sweet as honey." [10]I took the small scroll from the angel's hand and swallowed it. In my mouth it was like sweet honey, but when I had eaten it, my stomach turned sour. [11]Then someone said to me, "You must prophesy again about many peoples, nations, tongues, and kings."   **Revelation 10:1-11**

✧ ✧ ✧

We expect the seventh trumpet, but as happened before there is a pause. These interruptions not only increase suspense, they interlock portions of the book as flashbacks to earlier themes or as anticipations of what is to come. Even more importantly, they give us a key to John's personal theology in a way that the traditional forms and imagery in the numbered visions do not.

There are evident flashbacks here. In Chapter 1, John was told to prophesy (1:3, 19). Here he is told to prophesy again (10:11), indicating we are approaching the second part of the book. In Chapter 5 there was a mighty angel with a great scroll that was sealed; the Lamb takes the scroll and opens it. Here another mighty angel appears with a little scroll, already opened; the seer takes the scroll and eats it (10:9-10).

Is this angel actually the Son of Man who appeared in Chapter 1? Some elements suggest this. The cloud is a symbol of God's presence. The halo or rainbow is a symbol of his holiness or his mercy. His face, like that of Jesus in 1:16, shines like the sun (10:1). Caird has suggested that his legs like pillars of fire may signal that he will lead a new Exodus, for in the old Exodus the Lord led his people through the night by a pillar of fire. He stands on both land and sea (10:2, 8); he is master of the whole world (cf. Mt 28:18). When God speaks through a prophetic voice, it is like a lion roaring (10:3; cf. Am 1:2; 3:8; Jl 4:16; Hos 11:10).

Are we at a point in the development of the tradition where the spirit of prophecy is believed to be the angel of the risen Jesus? The scroll here (10:2) is not sealed but is already opened, an indication (as the angel will explain) that there will be no more delay. The Lamb's work of opening the seals is done. Now the plan of God is to be lived out by the church.

What are the seven thunders (10:3-4)? In Psalm 29, the manifestation of God in thunder is called seven times in succession "the voice of the Lord" (Ps 29:3-9). So it must be here. God affirms the revelation of the angel, which John the seer hears, but is not permitted to write down. This can mean either that revelation is limited (God will not tell human beings everything, but only what they need to know [Collins]); or it may mean that another series of woes that could have been released have been cancelled (Caird).

Amos (Am 7:1-6) received visions of woes that the Lord subsequently cancelled in answer to the prophet's prayer. In Mark 13:20 Jesus says, "If the Lord had not shortened those days, no one would be saved." This latter suggestion has much to commend it. In 10:6-7, the angel promises there will be no further delay in fulfilling "the mysterious plan of God." In modern private revelations (like Fatima and Medjugorje), there is often the revelation of secrets and the promise that impending chastisements can be tempered or removed by intense prayer and penance.

Like his predecessor Ezekiel (see Ez 3:1-4), John takes the scroll as directed and eats it (10:10). God's Word is not just something the prophet hears, it is something he devours: "When I found your words I devoured them; they became my joy and the happiness of my heart" (Jer 15:16). God's words become part of the prophet's very being. To Ezekiel and John they taste as sweet as honey, perhaps because they proclaim the ultimate victory of God.

Yet they also predict suffering both for the world and for the church, specifically here martyrdom (10:8-10). There is something fascinating here about the Word of God. God's Word, coming to the prophet, will announce suffering. Yet this suffering, like the cross of Jesus, will hasten the kingdom. Because it is God's permissive will, the Christian, like Jesus, can accept it and even find a deep sweetness in it.

Finally, John is told he must prophesy again (10:11). This points us forward to the rest of the book. The climactic word "kings" especially prepares us to meet the series of kings in 17:9-13, who will ultimately be conquered by the Lamb (17:14).

G G G

Reflection

Do our prayers have any effect on the course of world history? In our technological age we are often invited to think that human ingenuity eventually will be able to solve any problem. Human effort is all that is needed to apply it. But as the frontiers of the "impossible" recede, new problems appear. The perfect world constantly eludes human grasp. What we have just studied is a bold proclamation about the role of prayer in the unfolding of history and the achievement of God's kingdom. That unfolding awaits the intercessory prayer of the saints on earth.

When the events begin to happen, many are destructive, even of God's own creation. Is God an ecological terrorist? Hardly. History is made of God's good acts and men's and women's free choices. That is what the gift of free will means. God was asking for a messy world when he gave man and woman the freedom to choose. The cosmic disasters unleashed at each new trumpet blast are God's permission for the messy birthpangs of the new creation to begin. Those birthpangs are messy because they are a fusion of God's saving plan and human perversity. Is it surprising that modern technology, with its weapons of mass destruction, has made the replay of these visions a real possibility in our day? Because of humanity's abuse of free will, the world must inevitably go through a Good Friday. Nevertheless, God is there to assure that for those who cooperate with his saving plan there will be an Easter Sunday.

Questions

1. Why is there a half hour of silence in heaven?

They can hear the people on earth's prayers.
p. 129

2. Why do we not take vengeance into our own hands?

They could be interfering with Dads way of justice. p. 130

3. What sins of our generation will rain back on the earth? What can we do about it?

abortion, drugs. divorce bigotry,

4. Both opening the seals and sounding the trumpets brought suffering on the earth. How did they differ?

1 Seals - deal to the people on earth.
Trumpets - present some reality from a cosmic sense.

5. Why did John eat the small scroll? Why was it sweet?

He needed to evangelize.

6. How have I experienced the sweetness of God's Word?

7. How have I experienced the effect of prayer, especially intercession?

Prayer

Lord Jesus, when with you I pray to the Father, "Thy kingdom come," I tremble as I realize I am asking not only for the beauty, peace, and order that will eventually come but also for the cross and the purifying fire that must precede. Help me to realize the seriousness of that prayer. Give me the courage to accept and even welcome the birthpangs of the new creation. Amen.

SIX

The Suffering Church
(11:1–12:18)

T HE SUFFERING POOR have little luxury to worry about what is going to happen to the world at large. Those of more comfortable means perhaps are more prone to worry because a disturbance of world order means they would have to actually experience what the poorest of the poor experience daily. Within the church, it is a sign of spiritual maturity if we can get beyond even our spiritual self-interest and take on the corporate heart of the church. This is so often embodied for the modern world by apparitions of Mary weeping over the spiritual state of her children.

Several personal examples come to mind. Close friends of mine in a foreign country were beaten and imprisoned for their faith. In the spring of 1990 Judy, another close friend of mine working for peace in Northern Ireland, was wounded by an assassin's bullet. Walking with her was Timothy Dowling, who had dedicated his life to bringing the peace of Jesus to his country. The bullet that went through Judy's arm first passed through Tim, killing him instantly. Blessed Edith Stein was murdered by Hitler's henchmen. Many other Christians died the same way, including Father Jacob Gapp, an Austrian Marianist, who was beatified by Pope John Paul II in 1996. In this country some pro-life

Christians, who have engaged in Operation Rescue because of their conviction that babies are being murdered, have suffered police brutality.

Christians of all ages have found consolation in the Book of Revelation, particularly in those passages that deal with the suffering church. Such is the focus of the section of Revelation which we are now entering upon. It is the centerpiece of the book. In Chapters 11 and 12 John portrays the vocation of the church in two powerful images: the two witnesses and the woman.

THE MEASURING OF THE TEMPLE

[1]Then I was given a measuring rod like a staff and I was told, "Come and measure the temple of God and the altar, and count those who are worshiping in it. [2]But exclude the outer court of the temple; do not measure it, for it has been handed over to the Gentiles, who will trample the holy city for forty-two months. [3]I will commission my two witnesses to prophesy for those twelve hundred and sixty days, wearing sackcloth." [4]These are the two olive trees and the two lampstands that stand before the Lord of the earth. [5]If anyone wants to harm them, fire comes out of their mouths and devours their enemies. In this way, anyone wanting to harm them is sure to be slain. [6]They have the power to close up the sky so that no rain can fall during the time of their prophesying. They also have power to turn water into blood and to afflict the earth with any plague as often as they wish.

[7]When they have finished their testimony, the beast that comes up from the abyss will wage war against them and conquer them and kill them. [8]Their corpses will lie in the main street of the great city, which has the symbolic names "Sodom" and "Egypt," where indeed

their Lord was crucified. ⁹Those from every people, tribe, tongue, and nation will gaze on their corpses for three and a half days, and they will not allow their corpses to be buried. ¹⁰The inhabitants of the earth will gloat over them and be glad and exchange gifts because these two prophets tormented the inhabitants of the earth. ¹¹But after the three and a half days, a breath of life from God entered them. When they stood on their feet, great fear fell on those who saw them. ¹²Then they heard a loud voice from heaven say to them, "Come up here." So they went up to heaven in a cloud as their enemies looked on. ¹³At that moment there was a great earthquake, and a tenth of the city fell in ruins. Seven thousand people were killed during the earthquake; the rest were terrified and gave glory to the God of heaven.

¹⁴The second woe has passed, but the third is coming soon. Revelation 11:1-14

✧ ✧ ✧

If the modern reader finds this section of Revelation obscure, it has also been so for the biblical scholars. At first glance, 11:1-2 seem to imply that the Jerusalem temple is still standing, an argument for dating the book before A.D. 70. Some have suggested that this was originally a prophecy uttered during the Zealot occupation of the inner temple (during the Roman siege of the city). As a matter of fact, Titus, after burning the gates of the outer court, decided not to destroy the inner sanctuary. His soldiers got carried away by passion and set fire to it anyway. Whatever the origin of this saying, John—who elsewhere shows no interest whatsoever in the earthly Jerusalem or temple—has surely fashioned it to his purpose, no doubt applying it symbolically to the persecuted church of the A.D. 90s.

To *measure* (11:1) biblically can have various meanings. It can mean to mark for the purpose of rebuilding or destroying; but here its meaning is rather to seal for protection (as in 7:4-8). The temple, the altar, and the worshipers, therefore, represent the new people of God—the church which will be protected as it undergoes the great persecution. This trial (the trampling by the gentiles in 11:2) will last a short time—forty-two months (11:2), or twelve hundred and sixty days (11:3), or three-and-a-half years (12:14); they are all equivalent code numbers taken from Daniel (Dn 7:25; 12:7), meaning a brief period.

Even though many of them will have to die, the faithful will be secure because God has measured and sealed them. It is a paradox similar to the one in Luke 21:17-18: "They will put some of you to death ... but not a hair of your head will be destroyed." The point is that for a Christian, there is a difference between dying and being destroyed. He who loses his life for the Lord will preserve it for everlasting life (Mk 8:35).

Who are the two witnesses (11:3-12)? To understand this passage, as with many others in Revelation such as the previous one concerning the temple, it is important to understand the literary technique John is using here. It is an *overlay*— one or more scenes superimposed or run together to suggest that a current or imminent event is actually the meeting of several different motifs from the past.

We have seen this technique in the movies: a character's thoughts or dreams are portrayed while he is asleep. We know it from our own dreams, in which the raw materials may come from what we experienced the day before—but the drama and its meaning may be at an entirely different level. The popularity of the movie *Star Wars* was largely due to its use of well-known themes of previous plays or movies. T.S. Eliot made rich use of this technique in his poetry, using many biblical allusions.

So here we must distinguish the previous materials John is using from the *new thing* he is using them to designate. Thus the two witnesses evoke Moses and Elijah, representatives of the law and the prophets. They appeared with Jesus in the transfiguration and could have been thought to return before the coming of the Messiah (see Dt 18:15; Mal 3:23-24). The two olive trees and the two lampstands come from Zechariah's description of Joshua and Zerubbabel, leaders of the restoration after the exile (Zec 4:1-3, 11-14).

But what is the new and direct reference of these two witnesses? Are they Peter and Paul, who according to tradition were martyred in Rome? Are they all Christians who, like Zerubbabel and Joshua, are anointed kings and prophets (1:6; 3:12, 21; 20:6)? Probably we should take the fact that they are anonymous as an appeal to the reader to identify himself with them. We know of such a technique elsewhere in the Bible, that is, the nameless disciple of Matthew 8:21-22, or the anonymous "disciple whom Jesus loved" in the fourth Gospel.

The two witnesses are, therefore, the *readers* of Revelation who are invited to witness to God's work in the world, confident of his protection and his ultimate victory—which is also theirs, even should they have to endure a violent death. Like Elijah, they have the power to bring drought (11:6; 1 Kgs 17:1), or to bring fire from heaven (11:5; 1 Kgs 18:35-40; 2 Kgs 1:10). Like Moses, they have the power to turn water into blood (Ex 7:17-20), or to inflict any other plague (11:6). But like Jesus in the temptation and upon the cross, they do not use that power, however tempted they might be to do so. The fire which Elijah brought down from heaven comes from the *mouths* of the martyrs: their words before their pagan accusers (11:5). Like Jesus before the Sanhedrin and Pilate, they will by their faithful witness eventually bring down the pagan strongholds. But not before they give the supreme witness of martyrdom.

The code names "Sodom" and "Egypt" (11:8) do not stand for Jerusalem. Used seven more times in Revelation (16:19; 17:18; 18:10,16,18,19,21), "the great city" always means Rome. "Their Lord" was crucified *outside* the city of

Jerusalem but *within* the city limits of Rome, which were understood to embrace the entire empire. The ungodly will gloat over the death of the martyr-witnesses. After a short time they will be raised up and taken to heaven like Elijah (2 Kgs 2:11; see also 20:1-6).

The violent earthquake (11:13) is the concluding act of the drama introduced by the sixth trumpet, just as an earthquake occurred at the sixth seal (6:12). Here the phenomenon is a direct effect of the martyrs' death and glorification, similar to the earthquake that accompanied Jesus' death and resurrection (Mt 27:51; 28:2). Though a cosmic sign, it involves only a small portion of the city and its inhabitants, some of whom are converted ("gave glory to the God of heaven," see 11:13; elsewhere this means the positive sense of adoration: 14:7; 15:4; 16:9).

Thus in John's view, after the death and glorification of the martyrs, there will be a period in which the effects of their witness will be felt by the world. There will be large numbers of conversions. In this, the mystery of Jesus' own death is relived, for at the earthquake, the centurion and the other gentile guards at the crucifixion make the Christian confession, "Truly, this was the Son of God" (Mt 27:54). John did not live to see the complete fulfillment of his vision in the thousands of conversions that followed the great persecutions. Nonetheless his prophecy was fulfilled.

After the first four trumpets, the angel had announced that the last three trumpets would each bring a woe (8:13). The seventh trumpet is about to blow; therefore it will present the last of the three woes (11:14).

SOUNDING THE FINAL TRUMPET

¹⁵Then the seventh angel blew his trumpet. There were loud voices in heaven, saying, "The kingdom of the world now belongs to our Lord and to his Anointed, and

he will reign forever and ever." [16]The twenty-four elders who sat on their thrones before God prostrated themselves and worshiped God [17]and said:

> "We give thanks to you, Lord God almighty,
>   who are and who were.
> For you have assumed your great power
>   and have established your reign.
> [18]The nations raged,
>   but your wrath has come,
>   and the time for the dead to be judged,
> and to recompense your servants, the prophets,
>   and the holy ones and those who fear your name,
>   the small and the great alike,
> and to destroy those who destroy the earth."

[19]Then God's temple in heaven was opened, and the ark of his covenant could be seen in the temple. There were flashes of lightning, rumblings, and peals of thunder, an earthquake, and a violent hailstorm.

Revelation 11:15-19

✧ ✧ ✧

According to some scholars, this hymn, which expresses the main theme of Revelation, was intended by its author to be the center of the book. Indeed it celebrates the ultimate victory of God and his Anointed One, Christ. We might hear Handel's "Hallelujah Chorus" in the background: "The kingdom of this world is become the kingdom of our Lord and of his Christ." But the hymn is not the climax of Revelation, for we are only halfway through the book. There is much cosmic drama and conflict to come. Moreover, how can this glorious scene be the third woe announced in 11:14?

We are on safer ground if we see the interlocking technique at work once again. The *woe* of 11:14 and the seventh trumpet introduce a scene that not only concludes the preceding six but also opens up another series. In the process it gives us the key to their ultimate meaning, which will be climactically celebrated in the triumphal scenes of Chapters 20-22. This hymn then is an anticipation of the final victory, an interlude preparing us for the series of unnumbered visions.

While the worship is carried on in heaven, the kingdom is on earth. It *now* belongs to God and Christ (11:15). Obviously this is an anticipation of the ultimate victory, possible because in heaven, past and future all meld into the present. Psalm 2, one of the most important messianic psalms, forms the background music for much of this entire scene: it speaks of the "Lord and his Anointed" against whom the kings of the earth rise up (Ps 2:2; Rv 11:15), of the raging of the nations and the just wrath of God (Ps 2:1, 5, 11; Rv 11:18), and of the enthronement of the Messiah as king of all the earth (Ps 2:7-8).

To this John adds:

1. the judgment of the dead (11:18): the vindication of the martyrs;

2. the recompense of the Christian prophets;

3. the reward of the *holy ones:* the faithful who were spared martyrdom;

4. "those who fear your name," a term used in 11:13 above for nonbelievers who converted on seeing the death and glorification of the martyrs and the accompanying apocalyptic signs. The expression is borrowed literally from Psalm 115:13: "He will bless those who fear the Lord, both the small and the great." These are the "workers of the last hour" whose final repentance brought them into the kingdom.

5. The last item in 11:18 merits attention: "to destroy those who destroy the earth." Though we have met

much destruction and will meet more, it is not God's plan to destroy any of his creation. On the contrary, the destruction of his work comes from elsewhere, from sin and malice, led and abetted by the demonic "destroyers," of whom we have met: death and hades (6:8), the blazing mountain (8:8), the fallen star Wormwood (8:11), the angel of the abyss named "Destroyer" (9:11), and the Beast that rises from the abyss (11:7). In an age of increasing ecological awareness, this statement has a new and powerful meaning.

Finally, the heavenly ark of the covenant is revealed (11:19). It is the celestial counterpart of the earthly ark, which was concealed behind the curtain of the Holy of Holies, and could be approached only by the high priest once a year, on the Feast of the Atonement. Trumpets were blown on the feast. Here, after the blowing of the seventh trumpet, there is no more curtain, for the ark is revealed to everyone. It is the symbol of God's covenant fidelity and his presence in the midst of the faithful in glory. Or to put it more simply in the words of Jacques Ellul, the ark is the heart of God.

THE WOMAN AND THE DRAGON MEET

[1]A great sign appeared in the sky, a woman clothed with the sun, with the moon under her feet, and on her head a crown of twelve stars. [2]She was with child and wailed aloud in pain as she labored to give birth. [3]Then another sign appeared in the sky; it was a huge red dragon, with seven heads and ten horns, and on its heads were seven diadems. [4]Its tail swept away a third of the stars in the sky and hurled them down to the earth. Then the dragon stood before the woman about to give birth, to devour her child when she gave birth. [5]She gave birth to

a son, a male child, destined to rule all the nations with an iron rod. Her child was caught up to God and his throne. ⁶The woman herself fled into the desert where she had a place prepared by God, that there she might be taken care of for twelve hundred and sixty days.

⁷Then war broke out in heaven; Michael and his angels battled against the dragon. The dragon and its angels fought back, ⁸but they did not prevail and there was no longer any place for them in heaven. ⁹The huge dragon, the ancient serpent, who is called the Devil and Satan, who deceived the whole world, was thrown down to earth, and its angels were thrown down with it.

¹⁰Then I heard a loud voice in heaven say:

"Now have salvation and power come,
    and the kingdom of our God
    and the authority of his Anointed.
For the accuser of our brothers is cast out,
    who accuses them before our God day and night.
¹¹They conquered him by the blood of the Lamb
    and by the word of their testimony;
    love for life did not deter them from death.
¹²Therefore, rejoice, you heavens,
    and you who dwell in them.
But woe to you, earth and sea,
    for the Devil has come down to you in great fury,
    for he knows he has but a short time."

¹³When the dragon saw that it had been thrown down to the earth, it pursued the woman who had given birth to the male child. ¹⁴But the woman was given the two wings of the great eagle, so that she could fly to her place in the desert, where, far from the serpent, she was taken care of for a year, two years, and a half-year. ¹⁵The serpent, however, spewed a torrent of water out of his mouth after the woman to sweep her away with the current. ¹⁶But the earth helped the woman and opened its

mouth and swallowed the flood that the dragon spewed out of its mouth. [17]Then the dragon became angry with the woman and went off to wage war against the rest of her offspring, those who keep God's commandments and bear witness to Jesus. [18]It took its position on the sand of the sea.

Revelation 12:1-18

✧ ✧ ✧

This scene not only occupies the center of the Book of Revelation, but it also reveals with greater clarity the message of the writer. The identity of the persecutor becomes clearer, but so does the certainty of God's victory.

The Babylonians, Persians, Greeks, and Egyptians shared an ancient myth concerning a woman about to give birth to a prince or a new king. She is confronted by a monster or dragon seeking to destroy the child. The woman flees to safety; ultimately her child slays the dragon. By New Testament times, this myth was known throughout the empire. As the priestly author of Genesis had tailored the Babylonian creation myth to his monotheistic purpose, so John here selects some elements of the woman-child-dragon myth, fuses them with similar biblical figures, and applies them to the present situation of Christians. The victory is already settled in the heavenly war, thus assuring the final triumph in the church's continuing struggle on earth.

John does not call what he sees a vision but a *sign* (12:1), thus evoking the sign God himself promised to give to the faithless King Ahaz (Is 7:10-14). There the sign was of the maiden who would bring forth a son, the future king, and name him Immanuel ("God with us"). Isaiah probably had in mind Ahaz's young bride, Abijah, who would give birth to Hezekiah, in whom the prophet hoped the promises God made to David's dynasty could be fulfilled (2 Sam 7:8-16). Though the birth of Hezekiah brought great rejoicing and promise (Is 9:1-6), Isaiah became disillusioned even with Hezekiah and prophesied that only in a distant future king would God's perfect kingdom be realized (Is 11:1-9). Christians understood these prophecies to be fulfilled in Jesus' birth from the Virgin Mary (Mt 1:23). So we cannot totally exclude the birth of the individual Messiah, Jesus, and his mother from the present picture.

But other details suggest a different level of meaning to the "woman." Many passages of the Old Testament speak of Jerusalem as woman. She is "Daughter Jerusalem," "Daughter Zion," "Virgin Daughter," but especially *Mother.* Psalm 87 sings with pride that all Jews, including those of the diaspora, are really born in her: they claim her as their mother. But in time of suffering and exile, she is also a mother who weeps for her children (Jer 31:15; Lam 1:16; Is 51:18-20; Bar 4:5-29).

In a variation on this theme, the woman in the pains of childbirth is a collective image of the people suffering and longing for salvation: "As a woman about to give birth writhes and cries out in her pains, so were we in your presence, O Lord. We conceived and writhed in pain" (Is 26:17-18). The pains of childbirth thus become a stock image for the suffering of the entire people. Suffering, yes, but with the promise that new life will come about: "You will weep and mourn, while the world rejoices; you will grieve, but your grief will become joy. When a woman is in labor, she is in anguish because her hour has arrived; but when she has given birth to a child, she no longer remembers the pain because of her joy that a child has been born into the world" (Jn 16:20-21). Jesus spoke thus of his own redemptive suffering, forecasting what the disciples would also experience.

The woman then is a collective image of God's people suffering as a new birth is about to take place. The author makes no distinction here between the people of the Old Testament and those of the New Testament. The woman represents one continuous mystery of God working through his people to achieve his purposes. Though surely not meant to be understood as a goddess, this woman is invested with divine glory. She is clothed with the sun (compare the transfiguration of Jesus, in Mt 17:2). The moon has various symbolic values in the Bible:

1. a sign of permanence (Ps 72:7; 89:38);

2. a source of harmful rays (Ps 121:6);

3. a sign of the day of the Lord when it is eclipsed (Is 13:10; Ez 32:7; Jl 3:15; Mt 24:29; Mk 13:24), or when it turns blood-color (Jl 2:31; Acts 2:20; Rv 6:12).

Although Isaiah (30:26) said that in the messianic restoration the light of the moon would be as bright as the sun, 21:23 states that there will be no need for the moon because of the perpetual daylight in the heavenly Jerusalem. Which of these symbolisms fits the author's meaning here?

The moon was widely worshiped, not only by a number of Semitic peoples but also at times by Israel (Dt 4:19; 2 Kgs 23:5; Jb 31:26; Jer 8:2). Since John sees the moon, like the sea, no longer in the heavenly Jerusalem (21:23), it seems likely that the woman here stands on the moon as a symbol of ultimate conquest over the world's idolatry. The twelve stars in Jewish tradition would stand not for the zodiac but for the tribes of Israel. In a dream, Jacob's son Joseph saw the sun, moon, and eleven stars bowing down to him (Gn 37:9-10). In the synoptic tradition, the twelve apostles take the place of the twelve tribes of Israel (Mt 19:28; Lk 22:30). This woman, then, enveloped in divine glory, is both Mother Jerusalem (cf. Gal 4:26) and the New Testament church. Her sufferings (12:2) are persecution and martyrdom. Her cry is intercession to God to bring about the new birth promised in her pangs.

But this happy issue is threatened by the second sign appearing in the sky. In Chinese culture, the dragon is a symbol of grace. In biblical tradition, it evokes the "ancient Serpent" of Genesis 3, the "deceiver of the whole world" (12:9). Behind it lies the ancient pagan creation myth, whereby the monster of the watery abyss (Tiamat or Lotan) is conquered by the creator God.

In the poetic works of the Bible, the dragon appears as Leviathan or Rahab, the sea monster who embodies the forces of chaos and is driven into order by the creative Word of God (Ps 74:14; Is 27:1; Jb 3:8; 7:12). Second Isaiah applies this to God's creative action in saving his people (Is 51:9-11), for the dragon also personified Israel's historical enemies: Nebuchadnezzar (Jer 51:34) and Pharaoh (Ez 29:3). Here the dragon's heads and horns represent its universal power (cf. Ps 74:14, where Leviathan has more than one head).

The dragon comes from the sky (12:3) but he sweeps a third of the cosmic powers to the earth (12:4). Here, as in the Book of Enoch, the fallen stars probably symbolize fallen angels. We are on the lower stage once more. The dragon faces the woman and is poised to devour her child. The child she delivers is "destined to rule all the nations with an iron rod" (12:5), a clear allusion to the messianic Psalm 2:9. We think at once of Jesus' birth through Mary. In the complex overlying imagery of John, it would be rash to exclude that meaning.

However, in John 16:21 Jesus had used the image of birth-pangs and childbirth to refer to his own passion and glorification. Early Christian preaching portrayed Jesus' resurrection as God begetting his Son (Acts 13:33, an application of Psalm 2:7) and Jesus' ascension as his enthronement as Messiah (Acts 2:36). This would suit the context well here, which speaks of the messianic offspring being caught up to God and to his throne.

The desert into which the woman flees (12:6) is the desert

of refuge and protection, like the desert of the Exodus where the Lord called and espoused (betrothed) his people. Elsewhere in the Bible, unclean animals and unholy spirits dwell in the desert (Is 13:20-22; 34:13-15; Lk 12:24; Mk 1:13). For John they dwell rather in the city of Rome, which covers the entire empire. The basic meaning, then, is that the church will be protected for the short time (1260 days) of the persecution.

The heavenly war is then engaged (12:7). Michael, the angelic defender of Israel (Dn 10:13, 21; 12:1; Jude 9), engages the dragon and its angels, casting them from heaven. However, here they are not cast into hell but to the earth (12:9) where the battle will be resumed. Up to this point the record of the battle is little different from scenes described in the pre-Christian literature of Qumran. But in the hymn that follows, we find a specifically Christian interpretation: the real victor was not Michael in heaven but Jesus on earth, the Lamb who conquered by the shedding of his blood (12:11). Jesus had spoken of his saving death as the hour when Satan would be cast out (Jn 12:31).

Here the martyrs already glorified celebrate in anticipation the victory of their brothers and sisters on earth (12:10), who will join them (6:11), having conquered Satan by "the blood of the Lamb." Jesus' death gave them the power to be faithful unto death, but they shared and extended the effects of his saving death by their own martyrdom: "the word of their testimony." To love and choose life was God's Word to his people of old (Dt 30:19). But since the death of the Maccabean heroes (Dn 12:2-3) and particularly the victorious death of Jesus, the love of this life alone has not deterred God's faithful from bearing the ultimate witness.

Satan is "the accuser" (12:10). In Job 1:6-12, he appears as the "lawyer for the other side" who tries to convince the heavenly court and God himself that Job should be condemned. To gather evidence to this end, he sets about testing Job, ultimately to no avail. So it is with God's people as a whole, and specifically the church of the martyrs. The counterpart to the accuser is the defender, the Holy Spirit— described in the fourth Gospel as the Paraclete, who prosecutes the world, proving it wrong in its rejection of Jesus and his disciples (Jn 16:7-11).

The angels and the saints in heaven rejoice because they know the victory has been won. However, the battle will continue on earth (12:12). More Christians will still be martyred (6:11), including those who are yet to die in the Lord (14:13), and other children of the woman whom the dragon will fight on earth (12:17).

After the interlude of heavenly liturgy (12:10-12), the scene returns to the conflict of Satan with the woman and her child (12:13). Like Israel carried to safety on eagle's wings (Ex 19:4; Dt 32:11), the church finds refuge in the desert. Does John here refer to the historical tradition reported by Eusebius (*History,* 3:5) that before the destruction of Jerusalem the Christians, warned by a prophecy, fled to Pella across the Jordan? If so, the woman here would mean the Jewish "mother" community, and her "other children" (12:17), the gentile church.

Since the serpent is the sea monster, his weapon is a torrent of water, intended to engulf the church. The earth, which opened its mouth to swallow the rebels against God in Numbers 16:33, now swallows the torrent of God's enemy instead (12:16). Neither the woman nor the child fight the dragon on its own terms. On earth Jesus absorbed the devil's violence on the cross; simultaneously he cast him from heaven. So now the martyrs, represented by the earth, absorb the dragon's violence; thus the church itself is spared.

The word "offspring" in 12:17 is the same word used in Genesis 3:15 for the "seed" of the woman who would crush the head of the serpent. Her first offspring is Jesus, the Messiah. The "rest" probably refers to the second or third generation Christians who face martyrdom. The dragon withdraws to its native habitat, the sea (12:18), from which he will call up the Beast to continue the battle.

At this point, we need to sum up the interpretation of this passage:

1. The woman is, at the first level, messianic Israel which brings forth the Messiah in the birth which is the cross and resurrection of Jesus.

2. Her first offspring is Jesus, the crucified and risen Messiah; she also brings forth the community of faithful witnesses, first the Jewish Christian community and then "her other children," the gentile Christians. As the birth of Jesus to risen glory was painful, so the birth of new children comes through the "birthpangs" of persecution and martyrdom.

3. Though Mary, the mother of Jesus, is not intended directly, there are two reasons for seeing her at least as one of the "overlays" of this scene:

   a) The Old Testament "sign" and other messianic prophecies envisaged an individual woman, mother of the King.

   b) In the calvary scene in John 19:25-27, she is addressed as "woman," concrete embodiment of Mother Zion bringing forth her new children, personified in the beloved disciple.

The only way we can make sense of the time frame of the church's suffering on the one hand and its glorious vindication on the other is to understand what kind of time we are talking about: it is time as experienced in prayer. The Psalms of Lamentation illustrate how a praying Jew could experience the succession of events differently from the sequence in everyday life. The lamenter generally begins by pouring out his grief, sometimes almost shockingly. But he brings that grief to God, and once it is handed over to God, an amazing transformation takes place: he knows his prayer is answered, so he begins already to thank God for the answer to his prayer. This progression is very clear in Psalm 22, of which Jesus prayed at least the first verse from the cross, "My God, my God, why have you forsaken me?" The prayer of grief continues unabated until it issues in a cry of faith, "You heard me!" (Ps 22:22). Though many translations are different, Fr. Francis Martin, a New Testament scholar, observed that the pointing of the Hebrew letters may indeed be read as I have translated. And then the psalmist proceeds to praise God's gift of life. This is exactly the sequence we have in Revelation. John experiences the ultimate victory but only in the brilliant breakthrough of faith. But that is enough for him, and for his readers, to motivate them to be faithful unto death.

✧ ✧ ✧

Reflection

John invites us to identify both with the witnesses and with the woman. There will be a cost to witnessing, a cost which for the martyrs was life itself. But what about the little deaths we fear to face: loss of reputation or discomfort which living the daily Christian life entails? The woman, the church, is the symbol of God's ultimate victory over all the forces of evil. Yet for a time she must endure the birthpangs of suffering. If we are her "other children," then we may expect both suffering and victory, both the cross and resurrection.

Questions

1. What does it mean "to measure"? How can we explain the difference between dying and being destroyed?

2. What does it mean to destroy those who destroy the earth?

3. Who is the woman giving birth to the child? Who or what is the dragon? How do we fit into that vision?

4. What is the significance of the interlude of heavenly liturgy in this passage?

5. Why is the desert portrayed as a place of refuge and protection for the woman?

6. What can I apply to my life from the meaning of these images? Can I identify with the woman in the desert and the martyrs in heaven?

Woman = Brings out
the messianic age
Woman - Mary bring us the
Messiah

Prayer

"They conquered him by the blood of the Lamb." Lord Jesus, true Lamb of God, in the shedding of your blood you cast out the Prince of this world. You call me to share in your victory every day of my life. When I am confronted by temptation, when I feel weak in the face of evil in the world, remind me that in your blood I can claim the victory. May I be truly a child of that woman you have redeemed, preserved, and made victorious by your blood. Amen.

SEVEN

The Beasts and the Lamb
(13:1–14:20)

W E NOW MEET TWO HIDEOUS BEASTS. What are we to make of the beast with seven heads and ten horns? And what of the head which is mortally wounded? Some fundamentalist Christians view the growing unity of the European Community as a fulfillment of this prophetic image. The Antichrist will be a leader of the EC who will be mortally wounded and miraculously recover! And what of those who buy and sell bearing the mark of the beast? Some Christians believe that this will be a computerized, cashless system set up by a one-world government ruled by the Antichrist. And what of the image of the Lamb with the 144,000 on Mount Zion? Is this the number of the redeemed? The appeal of these images among fundamentalist Christians is powerful. Before surmising what they mean today, it is important to look at the text itself and see what John may have meant by it.

Having lost the first round in its fight against the woman, the dragon summons reinforcements. The first corresponds to the ancient mythical Leviathan, beast of the sea (12:1-10); the second, Behemoth, the beast of the land (12:11-18).

Since what comes from the sea is foreign, we may assume that the first beast represents the Roman imperial authority. Since what comes from the land is native, we may assume the second beast represents the local Roman authorities, though they too merely represent the first beast and enforce its worship (12:12).

The Power of The Lamb

THE BEAST FROM THE SEA: LEVIATHAN

¹Then I saw a beast come out of the sea with ten horns and seven heads; on its horns were ten diadems, and on its heads blasphemous name[s]. ²The beast I saw was like a leopard, but it had feet like a bear's, and its mouth was like the mouth of a lion. To it the dragon gave its own power and throne, along with great authority. ³I saw that one of its heads seemed to have been mortally wounded, but this mortal wound was healed. Fascinated, the whole world followed after the beast. ⁴They worshiped the dragon because it gave its authority to the beast; they also worshiped the beast and said, "Who can compare with the beast or who can fight against it?"

⁵The beast was given a mouth uttering proud boasts and blasphemies, and it was given authority to act for forty-two months. ⁶It opened its mouth to utter blasphemies against God, blaspheming his name and his dwelling and those who dwell in heaven. ⁷It was also allowed to wage war against the holy ones and conquer them, and it was granted authority over every tribe, people, tongue, and nation. ⁸All the inhabitants of the earth will worship it, all whose names were not written from the foundation of the world in the book of life, which belongs to the Lamb who was slain.

⁹Whoever has ears ought to hear these words.

¹⁰Anyone destined for captivity goes into captivity.

Anyone destined to be slain by the sword shall be
slain by the sword.
Such is the faithful endurance of the holy ones.

Revelation 13:1-10

You may be killed, but not
♦♦♦ destroyed.

Daniel had described four successive empires as beasts (Dn
7:2-7). John uses traits from all four beasts, reversing their
order, to describe the beast of the sea (13:2). In Daniel the
fourth beast was the Greek empire. By New Testament
times, Jewish tradition applied it to Rome. The heads
crowned with diadems are the Roman emperors (13:1).
Some of these upon their death were declared divine by the
Roman senate. Others anticipated the honor by having the
title *Divus* ("divine") impressed on the coins of their reign.
Domitian (A.D. 81-96), under whom the great persecution of
Revelation was unleashed, announced that he wished to be
addressed as *Dominus et Deus,* Lord and God. The tendency
began with Augustus, whose Greek name, *Sebastos,* was a
claim to divinity. The blasphemous name or names (we are
not sure whether the original text was singular or plural) is
evidently an allusion to this divine claim of the emperors.

Of itself the image of the Beast would signify irrational
power. But here, empowered by the dragon, it becomes
demonic (13:2). Being mortally wounded yet healed (13:3),
it becomes a parody of Jesus. To whom does it refer? Nero
committed suicide by putting a knife to his own throat.
However, rumor had it that he had escaped beyond the eastern frontier of the Roman Empire to Parthia, from which he
would one day return triumphant. What John apparently
means is that Nero has come back in the person of the
present emperor, Domitian.

Divine worship is given to the emperor (the beast) and
through him to Satan (13:3-4). Rome had established peace

and order throughout the empire. Many saw this as a boon and a relief from the preceding chaos. John does not deny this benefit of the empire (it helped Christianity spread in the early days). However, carried away with its own success, Rome demands and gets divine worship. The same scenario was repeated when Hitler was welcomed to power in Germany because he relieved the preceding economic and social chaos. Then he assumed—and was given—virtually divine authority, with disastrous consequences. It is the supreme tactic of Satan to push something good to an extreme that becomes demonic and destructive, seducing by the very mask of good.

Rome's time of tyranny is limited (13:5). Its blasphemies are directed not only against God and his dwelling but also to "those who dwell in heaven" (13:6). This could be the heavenly host, of course. It is more likely the church on earth, for the text literally reads, "to blaspheme his name *and* his dwelling, those who dwell in heaven." Notice that the *and* comes before "his dwelling," so that "those who dwell in heaven" simply explains "his dwelling." Later the dwelling of God is that which comes to earth (21:3).

Here that dwelling is anticipated in the church, which already enjoys the citizenship of heaven (Phil 3:20). But this community is not to be spared martyrdom (13:7). Like the Lamb, the Christians will win by being conquered. In the Greek of 13:8 the expression "from the foundation of the world" comes at the very end right after "the Lamb who was slain." The New American Bible takes it as modifying "those whose names were written," meaning that God had predestined the elect from the creation of the world. The other meaning is just as likely, namely, that the "Lamb was slain from the foundation of the world." In this sense it was God's plan from the very beginning that the salvation of the world would take place through the Lamb, as in 1 Peter 1:19-20: "You were ransomed... with the precious blood of Christ as of a spotless unblemished lamb. He was known before the foundation of the world but revealed in the final time for you." To the mortally wounded beast that has returned (Domitian), God's answer is the risen Lamb that was slain.

The heart of John's teaching in this section is contained in 13:9-10. The poetic cadences, which recall Jeremiah 15:2 and Zechariah 13:9, are capable of two interpretations:

1. The Roman persecutor who has taken the sword will perish by the sword (cf. Mt 26:52).

2. Christians who are destined for captivity or martyrdom should not expect to escape it.

The immediate addition, "Such is the faithful endurance of the holy ones," strongly favors the second interpretation. It is in surrendering to inescapable violence, rather than reacting with violence, that the victory will be won. Christians called before the Roman authorities must not expect to be spared by a last-minute divine intervention.

Like Jesus upon the cross, the martyrs will win their victory neither by escape nor aggressive retaliation. To respond to violence with violence escalates violence. It is the way of the Lamb to absorb it in redeeming love.

THE BEAST FROM THE LAND: BEHEMOTH

[11]Then I saw another beast come up out of the earth; it had two horns like a lamb's but spoke like a dragon. [12]It wielded all the authority of the first beast in its sight and made the earth and its inhabitants worship the first beast, whose mortal wound had been healed. [13]It performed great signs, even making fire come down from heaven to earth in the sight of everyone. [14]It deceived the inhabitants of the earth with the signs it was allowed to perform in the sight of the first beast, telling

Christians – stamp of baptism.

them to make an image for the beast who had been wounded by the sword and revived. [15]It was then permitted to breathe life into the beast's image, so that the beast's image could speak and [could] have anyone who did not worship it put to death. [16]It forced all the people, small and great, rich and poor, free and slave, to be given a stamped image on their right hands or their foreheads, [17]so that no one could buy or sell except one who had the stamped image of the beast's name or the number that stood for its name.

[18]Wisdom is needed here; one who understands can calculate the number of the beast, for it is a number that stands for a person. His number is six hundred and sixty-six. **Revelation 13:11-18**

❖ ❖ ❖

The danger of the second beast is in its seduction. Like the wolf that comes in sheep's clothing, it resembles Christ the Lamb but the message it gives is demonic (13:11). Since it holds the authority of Rome (the first beast) and forces the people to idolatry (13:12), the second beast symbolizes the powerful local elite who hold not only political but priestly office. They impose the cult of emperor worship. The Beast seduces by working false signs, aping the works of prophets like Elijah who made fire come down from heaven (13:13), or performing tricks of ventriloquism which give a quasi-supernatural authority to the Beast's demands for divine worship (13:15).

The stamping of people (13:16) is a travesty of the sealing of the elect (7:1-8). Those who bear the seal of the Beast are marked for plagues (16:2) and eternal punishment (14:9-11). The Greek word here for seal (*charagma*) was used for images of the emperor stamped on coins. Mentioning the right hand and forehead is probably meant to symbolize a demonic reversal of the Jewish practice of wearing phylacteries on the forehead and leather straps on the left arm, both symbols of the worship of the living God of Israel.

The involvement of economic life (13:16-17) is probably more than symbolic. Since Roman coins bore the image and name of the emperor, often pictured as a god, the Zealots who rebelled against Rome in A.D. 66-70 held that such coins were idolatrous. At some point Christians too must have discussed the issue. Jesus' response to the question in Mark 13:13-17 could be read as permitting payment of taxes to Rome. But "what belongs to God" in that same teaching could also have been interpreted as divine honor wrongly given to Caesar on the coin. John seems to come down on the more conservative view—that using the coin of the realm was cooperation in idolatrous worship.

Various attempts have been made to explain the number 666 (13:18). If seven is the perfect biblical number, then 666 falls triply short of it, thus symbolizing the height of imperfection or evil. But the text says it is the name of a person. The best solution lies in the ancient practice of *gematria*, in which numbers were considered symbolic. In Hebrew as well as in Greek, letters of the alphabet were used for numbers. If such were the case in English, A = 1, B = 2, K = 10, L = 20, and so on. In Hebrew the letters for Caesar Nero add up precisely to 666. In our interpretation, the ruling Emperor Domitian, under whom persecution of the Christians broke out over the issue of emperor worship, is Nero returned.

THE LAMB AND HIS RANSOMED

[1]Then I looked and there was the Lamb standing on Mount Zion, and with him a hundred and forty-four thousand who had his name and his Father's name written on their foreheads. [2]I heard a sound from heaven like the sound of rushing water or a loud peal of thun-

der. The sound I heard was like that of harpists playing their harps. [3]They were singing [what seemed to be] a new hymn before the throne, before the four living creatures and the elders. No one could learn this hymn except the hundred and forty-four thousand who had been ransomed from the earth. [4]These are they who were not defiled with women; they are virgins and these are the ones who follow the Lamb wherever he goes. They have been ransomed as the firstfruits of the human race for God and the Lamb. [5]On their lips no deceit has been found; they are unblemished. Revelation 14:1-5

they were not
misinterpreted as adults

❖ ❖ ❖

At this point it is worth recalling that we are in the midst of the unnumbered visions, in which the heart of the book becomes increasingly clear. The first three visions, beginning with that of the woman in Chapter 12, pictured conflict and suffering for the elect and for the world. Now John sees the glory of the victory awaiting the martyrs. Against the background again of Psalm 2, in which the Lord proclaims to the nations that have rebelled against him and his Messiah, "I have set up my king on Zion, my holy mountain" (Ps 2:6), John shows that Jesus is not alone in this victory; he shares and relives it in the victory of his faithful witnesses.

The king, however, is a Lamb (as in 5:6). In deliberate contrast to the beasts from the sea and the land, he stands on the holy mount of God. Many interpretations have been given to the 144,000 (see Fiorenza, p. 182). To discover who they are, we should note that they are numbered and they alone know the new song. They are the "firstfruits" and therefore are not the final harvest of the elect. Consequently, it is unlikely that they stand for all the faithful. Rather, the most probable meaning is that they are the same group as the 144,000 mentioned in 7:4-8: the martyrs. In 3:12 the risen Lord had promised that he would inscribe his name and the name of his Father on the victor. Here that promise is seen fulfilled (14:1).

To convey an idea of the sound of the heavenly choir, John combines the symbols of rushing water (we might think of a mighty waterfall) and thunder—obvious images of power—with that of harps, conveying gentleness and beauty. The new song (14:3) is the same as that sung by the heavenly choir to hail the victory of the Lamb in 5:9, later sung by the victors themselves in 7:10 where there is a vision of the anticipated bliss of the martyrs who pass through the great tribulation. Anyone who has been impressed with the beauty of a Bach chorale knows how difficult it is to learn. Here only those who can learn are counted among the 144,000 who have been "ransomed from the earth."

Obviously all Christians have been ransomed, but the martyrs' ransom is unique in that they have shared in the Lamb's own violent death. They alone know how to sing the song, meaning that the grace of martyrdom is unique. By applying to the martyrs, however, an expression that holds for all Christians ("ransomed from the earth"), John shows his high esteem for the martyrs. He also lays the foundation for the feeling widely shared in the succeeding decades that only the martyrs were "first class citizens" and the consequent thirst for the grace of joining Christ—even to the shedding of blood (see above on 2:10).

Verse 14:4 is difficult. At first sight it seems sexist. Are the 144,000 martyrs only celibate men? Were there no women martyrs? Were there no married martyrs? Is sexual intercourse "defiling"?

Such interpretations would put the Apocalypse at odds with the teaching of the New Testament elsewhere. Scholars have offered various solutions: 1) A later scribe who had a negative view of marriage inserted this into the text—a solution for which there is no textual evidence. 2) The language, as elsewhere in Revelation, is symbolic. This has much in its favor, since both in the Old Testament and in Revelation fornication is often used as a symbol of idolatry (Ez 16:1-58; 23:1-49; Rev 2:14-15, 20-22; 17:1-6). Virginity here then symbolizes fidelity to the covenant with the Lord. 3) A simpler solution, not entirely foreign to the preceding one: John is alluding to another well-known Jewish apocalyptic writing, 1 Enoch, which in the "Book of Watchers (Angels)," Chapters 1-36, refers to the angelic beings of Genesis 6:1-4 who defiled themselves by having intercourse with mortal women and thus fell from heaven. Hence 14:4 would mean that the faithful martyrs are now companions of the angels who did *not* sin. The fact that in their heavenly state they are "virgins" may echo Jesus' teaching that in heaven there is no marriage but that the faithful are like angels (Mt 22:30; Mk 12:25; Lk 20:35-36), a teaching which inspired many Christians to embrace celibacy for the kingdom even here on earth. But the text here is not saying that only those who were virgins on earth will follow the Lamb. It refers to all who remained faithful under martyrdom, who did not sin by infidelity as did the fallen angels.

In ancient Israel the offering of the firstfruits was a way of confessing that the entire crop was a gift of the Lord; thus it belonged to him. So too with the consecration of the firstborn. Offered to God by their parents, the firstborn could be redeemed, because the priestly order of the Levites took their place offering the perpetual worship of the entire people (Nm 8:14-19). Jesus was the firstfruits of the resurrection of all the just (1 Cor 15:20, 23). The Holy Spirit is called the firstfruits because he is the beginning of the fuller life to come (Rom 8:23; 2 Cor 1:22; 5:5; Eph 1:15). So here the martyrs, like the Levites, perform a priestly function for the entire people of God and the human race (1:6; 5:10). They are the herald and the promise of the great harvest of souls yet to come. Here again we encounter John's persistent theme that the sacrifice of the martyrs will have a redeeming effect on earth.

Of all the sins of which they are innocent, John singles out deceit (14:5). It is mentioned again in 21:7 and 22:15 as one of the vices that excludes from the New Jerusalem. Perhaps John is alluding to those who claim to be Jews but are not (3:9), or to the second beast, the false prophet (16:13; 19:20; 20:10), or to those who have apostatized, denying their Christian profession. More likely, however, he wishes to evoke Jesus, the Suffering Servant who had never spoken any falsehood (Is 53:9). Like an innocent lamb led to the slaughter, he atoned for the sins of the many (1 Pt 2:22-24). The martyrs relive the same mystery. The Lamb was without blemish (1 Pt 1:19), and so are they. This statement underlies the Catholic belief that the martyrs need no further purification in order to enter directly into the presence of God. Martyrdom is equivalent to canonization.

MEANWHILE ON EARTH...

⁶Then I saw another angel flying high overhead, with everlasting good news to announce to those who dwell on earth, to every nation, tribe, tongue, and people. ⁷He said in a loud voice, "Fear God and give him glory, for his time has come to sit in judgment. Worship him who made heaven and earth and sea and springs of water."

⁸A second angel followed, saying:
"Fallen, fallen is Babylon the great, *symbol of Rome*
   that made all the nations drink
   the wine of her licentious passion."

⁹A third angel followed them and said in a loud voice, "Anyone who worships the beast or its image, or accepts its mark on forehead or hand, ¹⁰will also drink the wine of God's fury, poured full strength into the cup of his wrath, and will be tormented in burning sulfur before

the holy angels and before the Lamb. [11]The smoke of the fire that torments them will rise forever and ever, and there will be no relief day or night for those who worship the beast or its image or accept the mark of its name." [12]Here is what sustains the holy ones who keep God's commandments and their faith in Jesus.

[13]I heard a voice from heaven say, "Write this: Blessed are the dead who die in the Lord from now on." "Yes," said the Spirit, "let them find rest from their labors, for their works accompany them." **Revelation 14:6-13**

✧ ✧ ✧

As is typical of John's style, the same mystery portrayed above in the heavenly vision of victory of the Lamb and the martyrs is now interpreted in events on the earthly stage. The first angel proclaims *everlasting good news* (14:6). For the first readers of Revelation, this would surely mean the preaching of the gospel to all the nations. Paradoxically, this good news is also news of judgment, the judgment of God's love for the world in the cross, as well as the effect upon those who by refusing the light choose darkness and self-destruction. God is presented through the image of Creator (14:7), for his good news can be in some way perceived by all peoples even in creation (cf. Rom 1:19-21). Even Christians begin their creed, "I believe in God... Creator of heaven and earth." But there is something remarkable here: the preaching of the good news is really done by the martyrs, who continue the witness of the cross to the nations. The blood of the martyrs, empowered by that of Jesus, proclaims the gospel to the world.

A second effect of the martyrs' sacrifice is portrayed by the second angel (14:8). John looks backward to the fall of ancient Babylon in the words of Isaiah 21:9, then forward to the fall of contemporary Babylon (Rome), which will be sung in greater detail in 18:1-19:4.

The third angel proclaims a warning to all (14:9-11). There is still time for repentance, but an awful fate awaits those who do not accept the grace. "Burning sulfur" is the fire and brimstone that destroyed Sodom and Gomorrah (Gn 19:24; Lk 17:29), with Sodom being another code name for Rome (14:8). Though the punishment is eternal (14:11), note that the sulfur burns before God and the Lamb, not before the Christians. The latter are not being invited to rejoice in personal vengeance upon their enemies.

But the certainty of God's victory and final judgment sustains the Christians who keep God's commandments and their faith in Jesus, the first martyr (14:12). Those who are called to die in the Lord in the persecution about to break out ("from now on") are blessed not merely because of the single work of martyrdom but because of their *works*—the plural indicating other good works as well. John shared the common Jewish belief that one's good works in this life followed the believer as witnesses on his behalf before the judgment court of God. Thus even those faithful not called to martyrdom share in this blessing.

THE HARVEST OF THE EARTH

[14]Then I looked and there was a white cloud, and sitting on the cloud one who looked like a son of man, with a gold crown on his head and a sharp sickle in his hand. [15]Another angel came out of the temple, crying out in a loud voice to the one sitting on the cloud, "Use your sickle and reap the harvest, for the time to reap has come, because the earth's harvest is fully ripe." [16]So the one who was sitting on the cloud swung his sickle over the earth, and the earth was harvested.

[17]Then another angel came out of the temple in heaven who also had a sharp sickle. [18]Then another angel

[came] from the altar, [who] was in charge of the fire, and cried out in a loud voice to the one who had the sharp sickle, "Use your sharp sickle and cut the clusters from the earth's vines, for its grapes are ripe." [19]So the angel swung his sickle over the earth and cut the earth's vintage. He threw it into the great wine press of God's fury. [20]The wine press was trodden outside the city and blood poured out of the wine press to the height of a horse's bridle for two hundred miles.   Revelation 14:14-20

We are now given two harvest images: one of grain, the other of grapes. In Jewish tradition, both were used as metaphors of God's judgment, either on his own people (Hos 6:11; Lam 1:15) or on their enemies (Jer 51:33). In Joel 3:13, the images are combined to describe the judgment of all nations: "Apply the sickle, for the harvest is ripe; come and tread, for the wine press is full; the vats overflow, for great is their malice." The treading of the winepress (14:20) is graphically used by Isaiah 63:1-6 for the Lord bringing his judgment upon the nations without any help from his own people.

Some scholars have, therefore, thought that John has used both these images to describe the final victory of God over all his enemies. But there are problems with this interpretation. In the Greek Old Testament, the noun *therismos* for harvest and its corresponding verb are never used for the mowing down of God's enemies. In the New Testament the harvest image is used in a joyful sense for the ingathering of the elect into the kingdom (Mt 9:37-38; Mk 4:29; Lk 10:2; Jn 4:35-38). The final coming of the Son of Man, who is apparently the figure described in 14:14, will be for this final ingathering (Mk 14:27). Furthermore, now that the first-fruits have been offered (14:4), the rest of the crop is ready to be reaped. Hence other authors, with better reason, see the first image as the final gathering of the elect in the final judgment.

Many of these same scholars go on to identify the image of the vintage (14:18-20) as God's final judgment upon the ungodly. They point out that, whereas the Son of Man reaps the grain, the judgment of the second group is delegated to an angel.

But there are problems with this interpretation as well. In 19:13-15, the Son of Man also treads the winepress. Here the harvesting is described as cutting the clusters from the earth's *vine* (remarkably *singular* in the Greek, not the plural as in the NAB). The vine was the Old Testament symbol for Israel. In the Johannine tradition it stands for Jesus and his members: "I am the vine, you are the branches" (Jn 15:5). Furthermore, the winepress is trodden "outside the city." In 18:4 those who remain inside the city share its sin and doom, while those who leave it will be protected.

If this is a judgment upon the city, we would rather expect it to be done within the city. Jesus was crucified outside the city walls (Mt 21:39), a fact that led the author of Hebrews to say: "Jesus also suffered outside the gate, to consecrate the people by his own blood. Let us then go to him outside the camp, bearing the reproach that he bore" (Heb 14:12-13).

We agree with Caird, then, that the second image, too, does not concern directly God's enemies but the blood shed by the martyrs in union with Jesus. The winepress is not yet the punishment of the persecutors, but the preparation of the drink that will make Babylon drunk (17:6; 18:6) and bring her downfall. To drink the blood of the martyrs is to drink the wrath of God.

The first image, then, concerns the harvest of all the elect, the second the blood shed by the martyrs. By combining the two images, John is relating the second to the first. The harvest of the elect has been won by the shedding of martyrs' blood, first the blood of Jesus, then the blood of those who suffer a violent death like his. Since the sea of blood is vast, John expects the number of martyrs to be many.

As we close this chapter, we may return to the questions with which we opened it. In reading all of this coded material, there is a great temptation to rush to an immediate contemporary reference. Of course it is the nature of symbols to lend themselves to multiple interpretations. And surely the beasts have been relived in various ways in the history of the church subsequent to the Roman Empire. But it is important to remember that the author had first in mind a specific historic situation—the imminent persecution of the church by Rome and the fate of the martyrs. The church reads Revelation as a message for our time, but the Holy Spirit does not guarantee our identification of contemporary counterparts as he did for John. The warning that is given, however, is the enduring one: when world powers oppress and seduce (the role of the two beasts), the church must resist and stand firm, even if it means being externally trampled. When called to martyrdom, Christians should know that theirs is a special grace, for it is a supreme way of sharing in the very passion and death of Jesus, which brought vindication by God, the reversal of this world's court verdict through resurrection, and redeeming grace for the world and even for the persecutor. The martyrs and the victorious Lamb can also inspire us in the little martyrdoms we endure in our daily fidelity to God who calls us.

❖ ❖ ❖

Reflection

Faith and baptism seal us in the Holy Spirit with the name of Jesus and the Father, or, as Revelation puts it, with the name of God and the Lamb. This is our ultimate identity. The world would like to claim us as its own. It would like to "mark" us with its own brand, removing our unique personhood and freedom and sweeping us into the enslaving worship of its values. Its two methods of "converting" us to itself are *fear* and *seduction*. We fall victim to the first beast when we yield to fear. We feel outnumbered and alone and decide that the easier way is to "go along" with what we do not really agree with in the depth of our faith-enlightened heart. We fall victim to the second beast when we let ourselves be so fascinated by the wonders of our technological age that we assume its consumerism, its narcissism, its hedonism, and its greed.

Questions

1. What is John telling us in the image of the sword in 13:9-10?

    p. 169

    Abound in love.

2. In contrast to the popular and literal meaning of the mark of the beast, what is its real significance?

    p. 170- 171

3. Are the ransomed of God, symbolized by the 144,000 and mentioned in Revelation 14, all martyrs and all celibate men? Is sexual intercourse "defiling"? What is John's meaning here? *p. 172*

    174

4. How should we respond to the scene of judgment in Revelation 14:6-13? Is it appropriate for Christians to seek vengeance? Or is this a sobering call to conversion and repentance before it is too late?

5. How are we to interpret the harvest of the earth in Revelation 14:14-20?

p. 178

p. 179

6. Is there an image or symbol in this chapter that has special relevance to my life? Why?

p. 177

Prayer

Father, I praise and thank you for your assurance of power and protection in the seal of my baptism. If ever I am called to give the ultimate witness to my faith, I trust that your grace will be there for me. In the meantime, grant that I may be faithful to the daily witness you call me to give in my home, my work, my church, and my civic community. May I know the joy of Jesus, who rejected the blandishments of the tempter and found his only delight in pleasing you. Amen.

chap 14:6

The Bowls of Wrath
(15:1–16:21)

G ET READY FOR MORE COSMIC DRAMA in what you are about to read. Chapter 16 of Revelation is considered by many fundamentalist Christians as a description of the final battle between the armies of the Antichrist and the Jews at Armageddon, signaling the end of the world. This is a very powerful and popular image, and it can fascinate our imagination and rivet our attention as much as *Star Wars* on an Imax screen. But is John really intending to give us a preview of an actual historical event, or does this scenario, melded from Old Testament images, have a deeper meaning for the Christian community of John's day—and for us? Does it have something to say about God's ultimate judgment on Satan's world-system and the call of Christians to persevere even to the shedding of their blood? Let us see.

THE FINAL PLAGUES

¹Then I saw in heaven another sign, great and awe-inspiring: seven angels with the seven last plagues, for through them God's fury is accomplished.
²Then I saw something like a sea of glass mingled with

fire. On the sea of glass were standing those who had won the victory over the beast and its image and the number that signified its name. They were holding God's harps, ³and they sang the song of Moses, the servant of God, and the song of the Lamb:

"Great and wonderful are your works,
   Lord God almighty.
Just and true are your ways,
   O king of the nations.
⁴Who will not fear you, Lord,
   or glorify your name?
For you alone are holy.
   All the nations will come
   and worship before you,
   for your righteous acts have been revealed."

⁵After this I had another vision. The temple that is the heavenly tent of testimony opened, ⁶and the seven angels with the seven plagues came out of the temple. They were dressed in clean white linen, with a gold sash around their chests. ⁷One of the four living creatures gave the seven angels seven gold bowls filled with the fury of God, who lives forever and ever. ⁸Then the temple became so filled with the smoke from God's glory and might that no one could enter it until the seven plagues of the seven angels had been accomplished.

Revelation 15:1-8

The last of the unnumbered visions introduces a new series of numbered visions. In them John returns to his more traditional imagery. The seven plagues belong to a scenario in which other themes of the old Exodus are used to describe the new Exodus: the sea, the song of Moses, the smoke of

Sinai, and the tent of testimony. To this we may add the fire of Sodom.

The final plagues will bring God's wrath to an end (15:1). Here again we must understand God's fury or anger as the inevitable effects of sin. For according to an equally biblical and even more authoritative text, Jesus says that God makes his sun to shine on the just and the unjust alike, and his rain to fall on the just and the unjust alike (Mt 5:45). This indicates that God loves his enemies. The wrath of God is what humans experience when they reject God's infinite love. It is felt in various trials or plagues. The reason that there are so many of them is that God, in great patience, is using them to call the rebellious to repentance. Still, our present text illustrates the horrors of the plagues themselves to show that the world's rebellion only proves the ultimate victory of God.

Before the plagues are presented, however, we are given another vision of the anticipated victory of the martyrs (15:2-4). They stand upon the sea of glass, which is now mingled with fire. In the first creation, God conquered the watery chaos by his word (Gn 1:1-3). That mystery was relived when the Lord brought the Israelites through the sea to the safety of the desert (Ex 14:10-31).

Now this sea is mixed with the fire of persecution and martyrdom, but the martyrs stand over it as victors (15:2). Just as the Israelites sang the "song of Moses" on the shore of the sea (Ex 15), the martyrs now sing the victory song of the Lamb (15:3-4). It is the combination of Jewish and Christian Passover imagery that will become the heritage of the Christian liturgy of Holy Week.

The hymn makes two important statements. God's saving action in history, like his past saving deeds (see Jgs 5:11), is described as his just or righteous deeds—his saving action in fidelity to his covenant promise to his people. Still, the result expected here is not the punishment of the nations but their conversion (15:4). As in 11:13 and 14:7, there is still hope that the sacrifice of the martyrs will bring about repentance and new life for the world.

The heavenly temple (containing the ark of the covenant) we have already seen in 11:19. Following the Greek Old Testament, it is called here the "tent of testimony" (i.e., the tent containing the tablets of the covenant), that mutual witness between God and his people, binding their lot and their future together. On earth the plagues will be experienced as punishment by the wicked. In heaven God is glorified because his saving justice is being accomplished. Recalling several Old Testament passages describing the temple so filled with the glory of God that it could not be entered, John affirms that the drama of salvation and judgment must be finished before access is possible to the heavenly temple.

THE SEVEN BOWLS

¹I heard a loud voice speaking from the temple to the seven angels, "Go and pour out the seven bowls of God's fury upon the earth."

²The first angel went and poured out his bowl on the earth. Festering and ugly sores broke out on those who had the mark of the beast or worshiped its image.

³The second angel poured out his bowl on the sea. The sea turned to blood like that from a corpse; every creature living in the sea died.

⁴The third angel poured out his bowl on the rivers and springs of water. These also turned to blood. ⁵Then I heard the angel in charge of the waters say:

"You are just, O Holy One,
    who are and who were,
    in passing this sentence.
⁶For they have shed the blood of the
    holy ones and the prophets,

and you [have] given them blood to drink;
it is what they deserve."

[7]Then I heard the altar cry out,

"Yes, Lord God almighty,
your judgments are true and just."

[8]The fourth angel poured out his bowl on the sun. It was given the power to burn people with fire. [9]People were burned by the scorching heat and blasphemed the name of God who had power over these plagues, but they did not repent or give him glory.

[10]The fifth angel poured out his bowl on the throne of the beast. Its kingdom was plunged into darkness, and people bit their tongues in pain [11]and blasphemed the God of heaven because of their pains and sores. But they did not repent of their works.

[12]The sixth angel emptied his bowl on the great river Euphrates. Its water was dried up to prepare the way for the kings of the East. [13]I saw three unclean spirits like frogs come from the mouth of the dragon, from the mouth of the beast, and from the mouth of the false prophet. [14]These were demonic spirits who performed signs. They went out to the kings of the whole world to assemble them from the battle on the great day of God the almighty. [15]("Behold, I am coming like a thief." Blessed is the one who watches and keeps his clothes ready, so that he may not go naked and people see him exposed.) [16]They then assembled the kings in the place that is named Armageddon in Hebrew.

[17]The seventh angel poured out his bowl into the air. A loud voice came out of the temple from the throne, saying, "It is done." [18]Then there were lightning flashes, rumblings, and peals of thunder, and a great earthquake. It was such a violent earthquake that there has never been one like it since the human race began on earth.

[19]The great city was split into three parts, and the gentile cities fell. But God remembered great Babylon, giving it the cup filled with the wine of his fury and wrath. [20]Every island fled, and mountains disappeared. [21]Large hailstones like huge weights came down from the sky on people, and they blasphemed God for the plague of hail because this plague was so severe. Revelation 16:1-21

❖ ❖ ❖

The plagues that now are visited upon the earth resemble those of the Exodus and those described earlier in the trumpet series (8:6-21). Several comments are appropriate here.

First, there is a solidarity of nature with the plans of God, so that nature itself experiences disturbance when human beings rebel against the author of nature. Shakespeare often played on this relationship, but long before him the Bible affirmed it. When Adam sins, the earth is cursed (Gn 3:17). That does not mean the Lord is displeased with the earth or intends to destroy it, rather that the elements of nature, having been witnesses to his covenant with the people of the earth, enforce retribution upon those who break it: "The earth is polluted because of its inhabitants, who have transgressed laws, violated statutes, broken the ancient covenant. *Therefore* a curse devours the earth, and its inhabitants pay for their guilt" (Is 24:5-6). The angel of the third plague states this explicitly (16:5-7). The Book of Wisdom affirms it clearly: "In return for their senseless, wicked thoughts... you sent upon them swarms of dumb creatures for vengeance; that they might recognize that a man is punished by the very things through which he sins" (Wis 11:15-16; see Wis 12:23, 27; Prv 1:31-32; 26:27).

Thus here, for example, the blood of the martyrs contaminates the persecutor's water supply (16:4-6). Of course, nature's retribution is not administered by the martyrs, for they never avenge themselves in Revelation. Rather, by divine permission, nature is enlisted by angels who pour out retribution from bowls. What the bowls contain is either the prayers of the saints or the blood of the martyrs (cf. 17:6), thus indicating again the effectiveness of intercession and martyrdom before the throne of God. As his agents, the angels indicate that, just as the persecutor's sin is not only murder but blasphemy against God, so too the punishment is a personal message from God to the persecutor.

Second, the message is still an appeal to repentance, as 16:11 clearly states. Cosmic plagues are followed by political ones, as the empire is plunged into darkness in the fifth plague (16:10-11). Not even this brings about repentance—instead, blasphemy. Indeed, until these plagues, blasphemy was the sin only of the Beast. Now that sin is aped by the persecutors (16:9, 11, 21).

The sixth plague (16:12-16) is the most detailed. The Euphrates was the eastern frontier of the empire, beyond which lay the Parthian armies. The sixth bowl dries up the river so that the armies may invade unimpeded to punish the idolaters of the Roman world (Lindsey interprets these armies here, as in 9:14-18, as those of Communist China). Recalling the frogs of the Exodus from Egypt, the unclean spirits come forth simultaneously from the dragon, the Beast, and the false prophet in a conspiracy of seduction. The kings of the earth unwittingly follow them to the staging ground for the final battle "on the great day of God the almighty." Armageddon (16:16) means literally "the hill of Megiddo," which is probably an eschatological projection of the memorable Jewish battlefield where Sisera was defeated (Jgs 5:19-21) and Kings Ahaziah and Josiah were slain (2 Kgs 9:27; 23:29). In Zechariah 12:11 it is called a plain. Actually it was a fortified city guarding a pass through which lay an arterial highway.

Some authorities understand the kings assembled there to be the same as the "kings of the East" of 16:12. But here they are the kings of the whole earth (16:14), so it is more likely that they are to witness and be judged by the King of Kings on his great day of final victory.

But 16:15 boldly intrudes on this description. So similar is this verse to the letters in Chapters 2 and 3 that some authorities think it is misplaced here. More likely, it is John's deliberate aside to his Christian readers to warn them that Jesus comes not only at the end of time but also in historical crises. There is a rare convergence here with the theology of Mark. In Mark, Jesus comes to his disciples not in a parousia but in the hour of suffering; it is for that coming they are not prepared (Mk 14:37-42). The young man who flees naked (Mk 14:51-52) symbolizes this unpreparedness, just as the young man clothed in a white robe at the tomb of the resurrection (Mk 16:5) represents restoration and sharing in Christ's glory.

Unlike the seventh seal and the seventh trumpet, there is no "cancelled conclusion" following the seventh bowl. No new series is opened up; instead, "it is done." The cosmic horrors at first sight suggest the end of the world, but since there are still people around to blaspheme (16:21) and spectators to lament (18:9-18), we must conclude that, as has happened before in the Bible, cosmic imagery has been used to describe a political disaster. The final collapse of the physical universe is still a long way off (20:11).

The fall of the great city, the disappearance of the mountains (evoking perhaps the seven hills of the harlot, 17:9), and the code name Babylon clearly refer to the collapse of Rome. We touch here once again an important key to interpreting apocalyptic literature. Just as the Old Testament prophets and Jesus himself used cosmic language to describe political events like the fall of a city (Is 13:10; Mk 13:24-25) or the death of a tyrant (Ez 32:7-8), just as Matthew used cosmic imagery to convey the changing of the ages at the death and resurrection of Jesus (Mt 27:51-54; 28:2), so

John, intending to foretell the "things that are to happen soon" (1:1), describes not the end of the world but the end of the Roman persecutor, the end of Rome's world.

What is the message of all this for us today? John, a Jew whose thought patterns have been shaped by a rich biblical tradition centered in the Exodus, has found yet another way of telling us that the future is in God's hands, that the prayers of the saints are a key factor in moving his kingdom to its fulfillment. The perversity of those who use their free will to resist God's plan of redeeming love makes the phases of that unfolding bitter and at times destructive. For them it is experienced as God's wrath because they have chosen it to be so. Today those who choose to live in the kingdom of death and destruction bring misery upon the saints on earth and upon themselves as well. One cannot promote death and destruction and escape what one promotes. The faithful too may have to pass through a sea of fire, but they will ultimately stand over it, while the kingdom of this world, to the extent that it is the kingdom of Satan, will be consumed.

✧ ✧ ✧

Reflection

Have I really understood the meaning of God's wrath? Perhaps I have thought of it as something arbitrary and vengeful. In reality it is God's love which is based on truth, which cannot let evil rule the world. He would prefer that it not rule any human heart. But he will not withdraw the freedom he has given his human creatures, because he wants from them the kind of response he cannot get from nature which follows his laws blindly. It is indeed a mystery, and the stakes for humanity are high.

Questions

1. What is meant by the martyrs standing upon the sea of glass which is now mingled with fire in 16:2-4?

2. What is the role of nature when humans sin?

3. Where does the sixth angel pour out his bowl and what are the results?

4. How does John use cosmic language to signify the end of an age?

5. How does this imagery apply to my life?

Prayer

Lord Jesus, by your blood you give me entrance to the heavenly liturgy, even as I pray here on earth. You have let me see that reality. My presence there is not meant to be merely decorative, but you wish my prayer to be joined with yours and that of the angels and saints. With you and all the heavenly hosts, I pray, "Thy kingdom come," assured that I am truly helping to advance the coming of your kingdom on earth. Increase my faith in the power of prayer. Amen.

NINE

Fall of Babylon and Her Godless Allies
(17:1–19:21)

J UST AS THERE HAS BEEN MUCH popular speculation about the identity of the Antichrist and the Beast, so with the harlot or whore of Babylon, whom we meet in this chapter. Certain fundamentalist Christians have even claimed that she is the Roman Catholic Church, which will be ruled over by the Antichrist, a future pope from Rome. Our analysis will show that such an interpretation not only misses what John meant by the harlot (and thus is historically inaccurate) but it obscures the crucial significance of this image for Christians today. For today, like the emperors of ancient Rome, many prostitute themselves to hedonistic and materialist values while the rest of the world suffers in misery, oppression, and want. This sort of lifestyle, which typifies the world-system of Satan, brings down the wrath of God. In this situation Christians are called to be countercultural witnesses to the truth of the gospel. Again, let us first listen to John in his own words.

THE HARLOT AND THE BEAST

[17]Then one of the seven angels who were holding the seven bowls came and said to me, "Come here. I will show you the judgment on the great harlot who lives near the many waters. [2]The kings of the earth have had intercourse with her, and the inhabitants of the earth became drunk on the wine of her harlotry." [3]Then he carried me away in spirit to a deserted place where I saw a woman seated on a scarlet beast that was covered with blasphemous names, with seven heads and ten horns. [4]The woman was wearing purple and scarlet and adorned with gold, precious stones, and pearls. She held in her hand a gold cup that was filled with the abominable and sordid deeds of her harlotry. [5]On her forehead was written a name, which is mystery, "Babylon the great, the mother of harlots and of the abominations of the earth." [6]I saw that the woman was drunk on the blood of the holy ones and on the blood of the witnesses to Jesus.

Revelation 17:1-6

✧ ✧ ✧

What follows now is really an elaboration of the preceding themes, as one of the angels holding the bowls presents a new vision. The punishment of Rome is described as a past event—very much like the "prophetic perfect" used by the Old Testament prophets to foretell a future event as having already happened (for in God's counsel it has and the outcome is certain).

Cities in the Bible were often personified as women: Jerusalem as virgin, daughter, mother, or widow, while the pagan cities and even Israel herself as prostitutes. Harlotry was chosen as a symbol of infidelity not only because the covenant union with the Lord was portrayed as an inviolable marriage. Ritual prostitution was often practiced in the pagan cults.

The harlot will be the antagonist and foil for the woman

of Chapter 12. Rome is again portrayed cryptically with the colors of ancient Babylon that sat beside the waters of its great irrigation systems (Jer 51:13). Applied to Rome, the image will be reinterpreted in 17:15 as "large numbers of peoples, nations and tongues." The kings of the earth (soon to be contrasted with the King of Kings, 19:11-16) and many of its inhabitants were seduced by her, that is, led into idolatry and emperor worship.

The harlot announced in 17:1 is not seen by John until he is taken to the desert (17:3). The desert is a place of refuge and discernment. In the surrounding culture, it is difficult for the church to see clearly with the eyes of God. Therefore she must periodically be led, as Jesus was, into the desert, which in this world is the church's only true home. The Beast (already mentioned in 13:1-10) is scarlet and seven-headed. It is explained in 17:9 as an allusion to the seven hills of Rome and seven emperors. The horns also stand for its emperors, while the blasphemous names stand for the divine titles assumed by them.

The harlot is extravagantly dressed—an allusion to the wealth of Rome—and though her cup is gold, it is filled with the filth of idolatry (17:4). Another obvious allusion to Rome, the Babylon of John's day, is found in 17:5. She has become drunk upon the blood of the saints and martyrs she has killed (17:6). As a result, she will become more and more irrational in her actions—to her own ultimate destruction.

INTERPRETATION OF THE HARLOT AND THE BEAST

[7]When I saw her I was greatly amazed. The angel said to me, "Why are you amazed? I will explain to you the mystery of the woman and of the beast that carries her, the beast with the seven heads and the ten horns. [8]The beast that you saw existed once but now exists no longer. It will come up from the abyss and is headed for destruc-

tion. The inhabitants of the earth whose names have not been written in the book of life from the foundation of the world shall be amazed when they see the beast, because it existed once but exists no longer, and yet it will come again. [9]Here is a clue for one who has wisdom. The seven heads represent seven hills upon which the woman sits. They also represent seven kings: [10]five have already fallen, one still lives, and the last has not yet come, and when he comes he must remain only a short while. [11]The beast that existed once but exists no longer is an eighth king, but really belongs to the seven and is headed for destruction. [12]The ten horns that you saw represent ten kings who have not yet been crowned; they will receive royal authority along with the beast for one hour. [13]They are of one mind and will give their power and authority to the beast. [14]They will fight with the Lamb, but the Lamb will conquer them, for he is Lord of lords and king of kings, and those with him are called, chosen, and faithful."

[15]Then he said to me, "The waters that you saw where the harlot lives represent large numbers of peoples, nations, and tongues. [16]The ten horns that you saw and the beast will hate the harlot; they will leave her desolate and naked; they will eat her flesh and consume her with fire. [17]For God has put it into their minds to carry out his purpose and to make them come to an agreement to give their kingdom to the beast until the words of God are accomplished. [18]The woman whom you saw represents the great city that has sovereignty over the kings of the earth." **Revelation 17:7-18**

❖ ❖ ❖

The Beast that existed once but will return (17:8) is doubtless an allusion to the popular belief that Nero would return at the head of the Parthian army to reclaim the

Roman Empire. John's enumeration of the five kings that have already come (17:10) probably begins with Caligula (A.D. 37-41). Known for his cruelty, he was the first to come into serious conflict with the Jews. He presented himself as a god in his own lifetime. He and his four successors "fell": Caligula was murdered, Claudius was poisoned, Nero committed suicide, and Vespasian and Titus died of fevers.

Domitian, the sixth king, is presently reigning. He will be followed by a seventh and even an eighth, who will be the Beast, Nero *redivivus*. This stands in some tension with our interpretation of 13:18, where it appeared that Domitian was Nero returned. Some scholars think the seven kings represent all the Roman emperors (seven being the number of completion). More than one emperor, of course, could look like Nero returned.

In any case, the present text foresees two more emperors after the present one. The ten kings have not yet been crowned (17:12); they are probably the little Parthian potentates who would, in the popular scenario, ally themselves with Nero in his reconquest of the empire (17:16-17). It is not clear whether the Beast's battle with the Lamb (17:14) will occur before or after the Beast's conquest of the harlot. The sequence of the text suggests that, before destroying the harlot, the Beast and his allies fight the Lamb by persecuting his followers. It seems that John has used the popular belief in Nero's return to teach a double lesson:

1. The Lamb will conquer in the person of his martyr-members.

2. The beast will destroy the harlot. The instrument for destroying the Lamb's enemies are the enemies themselves—a biblical theme that goes back at least as far as Gideon's conquest of the Midianites (Jgs 7:22). The enemies of God are ultimately their own worst enemies. They will eventually self-destruct.

THE FALL OF BABYLON

[1]After this I saw another angel coming down from heaven, having great authority, and the earth became illumined by his splendor. [2]He cried out in a mighty voice:

"Fallen, fallen is Babylon the great.
    She has become a haunt for demons.
She is a cage for every unclean spirit,
    a cage for every unclean bird,
    [a cage for every unclean] and disgusting [beast].
[3]For all the nations have drunk
    the wine of her licentious passion.
The kings of the earth had intercourse with her,
    and the merchants of the earth grew
        right from her drive for luxury."

[4]Then I heard another voice from heaven say:

"Depart from her, my people,
    so as not to take part in her sins
    and receive a share in her plagues,
[5]for her sins are piled up to the sky,
    and God remembers her crimes.
[6]Pay her back as she has paid others.
    Pay her back double for her deeds.
    Into her cup pour double what she poured.
[7]To the measure of her boasting and wantonness
    repay her in torment and grief;
for she said to herself,
    'I sit enthroned as queen;
    I am no widow,
    and I will never know grief.'
[8]Therefore, her plagues will come in one day,
    pestilence, grief, and famine;
    she will be consumed by fire.
For mighty is the Lord God who judges her."

⁹The kings of the earth who had intercourse with her in their wantonness will weep and mourn over her when they see the smoke of her pyre. ¹⁰They will keep their distance for fear of the torment inflicted on her, and they will say:

"Alas, alas, great city,
    Babylon, mighty city.
    In one hour your judgment has come."

¹¹The merchants of the earth will weep and mourn for her, because there will be no more markets for their cargo: ¹²their cargo of gold, silver, precious stones, and pearls; fine linen, purple silk, and scarlet cloth; fragrant wood of every kind, all articles of ivory and all articles of the most expensive wood, bronze, iron, and marble; ¹³cinnamon, spice, incense, myrrh, and frankincense; wine, olive oil, fine flour, and wheat; cattle and sheep, horses and chariots, and slaves, that is, human beings.

¹⁴"The fruit you craved
    has left you.
All your luxury and splendor are gone,
    never again will one find them."

¹⁵The merchants who deal in these goods, who grew rich from her, will keep their distance for fear of the torment inflicted on her. Weeping and mourning, ¹⁶they cry out:

"Alas, alas, great city,
    wearing fine linen, purple and scarlet,
    adorned [in] gold, precious stones, and pearls.
¹⁷In one hour this great wealth has been ruined."

Every captain of a ship, every traveler at sea, sailors, and seafaring merchants stood at a distance ¹⁸and cried out when they saw the smoke of her pyre, "What city

could compare with the great city?" ¹⁹They threw dust
on their heads and cried out, weeping and mourning:

"Alas, alas, great city,
    in which all who had ships at sea
    grew rich from her wealth.
In one hour she has been ruined.
²⁰Rejoice over her, heaven,
    you holy ones, apostles, and prophets.
For God has judged your case against her."

²¹A mighty angel picked up a stone like a huge millstone and threw it into the sea and said:

"With such force will Babylon the great
        city be thrown down,
    and will never be found again.
²²No melodies of harpists and musicians,
    flutists and trumpeters,
    will ever be heard in you again.
No craftsmen in any trade
    will ever be found in you again.
No sound of the millstone
    will ever be heard in you again.
²³No light from a lamp
    will ever be seen in you again.
No voices of bride and groom
    will ever be heard in you again.
Because your merchants were the great
        ones of the world,
    all nations were led astray by your magic potion.
²⁴In her was found the blood of prophets and holy
    ones and all who have been slain on the earth."

¹After this I heard what sounded like the loud voice of
a great multitude in heaven, saying:

"Alleluia!

Salvation, glory, and might belong to our God,
    [2]for true and just are his judgments.
He has condemned the great harlot
    who corrupted the earth with her harlotry.
He has avenged on her the blood of his servants."
[3]They said a second time:
    "Alleluia! Smoke will rise from her forever and ever."

[4]The twenty-four elders and the four living creatures
fell down and worshiped God who sat on the throne,
saying, "Amen. Alleluia."   Revelation 18:1-19:4

❖ ❖ ❖

This long section does not require a lengthy commentary.
We should note that some Christian groups have taken the
harlot here to stand, not for the Roman persecutors of the
first century Christians, but for "ecclesiastical Babylon." This
is sometimes interpreted as "all apostate Christendom, in
which the Papacy will undoubtedly be prominent" (Scofield
Bible). There are no scriptural grounds whatsoever for such
an interpretation. In Revelation, the whole church is under
the boot of the Roman persecutor. While there are false
prophets and weak members in its ranks, there is no suggestion whatever that a major *Christian* force is the enemy.

Following Old Testament patterns, this section is a series
of dirges or laments proclaiming the fall of pagan Rome
(Babylon) and celebrating God's judgment for her crimes.
Each scene represents a different response to the collapse of
the city which, as Adela Collins remarks, is happening as it
were offstage. There is also a frequent shift of speakers and
addressees. Similar dirges against oppressor cities are found
in Isaiah 23, 24, 27, Jeremiah 50-51, and Ezekiel 26-27.
The whole section is, of course, not a present reality but a
prophetic certainty.

In 18:2-3 note the reason for the fall of Rome is not

merely her persecution of Christians but her immorality. Like the drug and pornography lords of today, the merchants of the empire have let the lust for money draw them into licentious luxury, abandoning all social responsibility. In 18:4-5 it is not clear who the speaker is (whether God, Christ, or an angel), but the message is clearly addressed to Christians on earth. The expression "Depart from her" was used frequently in judgment threats of Isaiah (Is 48:20; 52:11) and Jeremiah (Jer 50:8; 51:6, 9, 45). But it was already interpreted by Paul (2 Cor 6:17) in the sense of a spiritual rather than a physical separation. Christians are not being encouraged, like the Essenes, to withdraw into a ghetto; still, John is worried about the economic ties of his wealthier communities to the social and religious fabric of the day (see commentary on 3:14-19). The essential message is: do not share Rome's sins lest you share her downfall.

It is not clear to whom 18:6-7 are addressed, nor does it greatly matter. The agents of the retribution are certainly not the Christians. Nowhere else in Revelation, or in the New Testament for that matter, are they invited to avenge themselves. We have seen that the avengers are at times the angels, and at times the very enemies of the church themselves (18:13-17). In 18:8, the key is given: it is the mighty God who is judging the wicked city.

But there are those who weep for Rome: first of all the kings of the earth who shared her misguided ways (18:9-10) and now seek to distance themselves from her plight. Unwittingly perhaps, they voice the Christian view as they conclude: "your judgment has come" (18:10).

The merchants reveal their self-interest in two ways:

1. like the kings, they try to distance themselves from the perishing city (18:15);

2. they moan the loss of their own markets, which included even slaves (18:11-17).

It is not God's judgment that they perceive (as did the kings in 18:10); they simply observe the ruin of the city's wealth (18:17). The seafaring peoples and merchants join in the lament in similar tones, but their proclamation of God's judgment is clearer than that of the kings (assuming 18:20 is voiced by the merchants). They congratulate the heavens, the saints, apostles, and prophets, "for God has judged your case against her." This is a surprising thing for the sea merchants to say, for surely they have profited by the commerce of Rome. Perhaps John means to signal that some portion of the business empire, like the centurion at the foot of the cross (Lk 23:47), would confess the justice of the oppressed and the reversal of lots.

Texts from Old Testament dirges (Jer 51:63-64; Ez 26:13, 21; Is 24:8) are now applied to Rome in 18:21-23. John himself does not weep over Rome as Jesus did over Jerusalem for its lack of repentance. However, there is a touch of awe, perhaps even of sorrow, on John's part as he reviews these tragic scenes. In 18:24 the reason for the reversal of her lot is given: not only the blood of prophets and the holy ones, but all the innocent who have been slain on the earth. John is not chauvinistic—the shedding of innocent blood, no matter to whom it belongs, cries to God for vengeance (Gn 4:10).

In contrast to the dismay, shock, and grief of kings, merchants, and sea merchants (which evokes the sober statement that the fall of Rome is God's just judgment), there is praise of God in heaven as the celestial chorus intones the "Alleluia" (19:1). In the New Testament this acclamation appears only four times, all four of them here (19:1, 3, 4, 6). The heavenly liturgy gives the ultimate interpretation of the historical event: God's justice has finally been done on earth. That is cause for rejoicing. The injustice of the oppressor has run its course— to its own undoing. The blood of the martyrs has not been shed in vain. Conversions have multiplied, and those who persisted in their oppression have tasted its bitter fruits.

VICTORY SONG AND WEDDING FEAST

⁵A voice coming from the throne said:

"Praise our God, all you his servants,
[and] you who revere him, small and great."

⁶Then I heard something like the sound of a great multitude or the sound of rushing water or mighty peals of thunder, as they said:

"Alleluia!
The Lord has established his reign,
[our] God, the almighty.
⁷Let us rejoice and be glad
and give him glory.
For the wedding day of the Lamb has come,
his bride has made herself ready.
⁸She was allowed to wear
a bright, clean linen garment."
(The linen represents the righteous deeds of the holy ones.)

⁹Then the angel said to me, "Write this: Blessed are those who have been called to the wedding feast of the Lamb." And he said to me, "These words are true; they come from God." ¹⁰I fell at his feet to worship him. But he said to me, "Don't! I am a fellow servant of yours and of your brothers who bear witness to Jesus. Worship God. Witness to Jesus is the spirit of prophecy."

Revelation 19:5-10

✧ ✧ ✧

To the heavenly Alleluias we have just heard (19:1-4), the heavenly voice now invites the participation of all God's servants, therefore those on earth as well as in heaven, those who have been martyred or will be, and those little ones

(11:18) who will not be called to this supreme sacrifice (19:5). This passage bears many similarities with that introduced by the seventh trumpet in 11:15-18. But now a new image is introduced.

The victory celebration is not described as a pronouncement of judgment. It is a wedding feast: the Lamb is the groom and the church is the bride (19:7-8). Already in the Old Testament, the promised kingdom of God was described as a feast (Is 25:6). This theme was repeated in Luke 14:15. It was described as a wedding banquet with Jesus the bridegroom in Mark 2:19; Matthew 22:1-14; 25:1-13. Like Israel of old (Hos 2:4-22; Is 1:21; 54:5-6; Jer 2:2; Ez 16:6-14), the church is the bride (2 Cor 11:2; Eph 5:27-32). The celebration of the wedding is presented here.

However, the celebration is not the moment when the Word became flesh, nor even the death and resurrection of Jesus, nor his ascension nor his sending of the Spirit, but the final union of the bride with her Spouse in glory. How has the bride "made herself ready"? By the blood of the martyrs, but also by the righteous deeds of all the saints. In the Old Testament, fresh clothes were a symbol of separation from the spiritually unclean; therefore holiness (Gn 35:2), whether of the priests (Zec 3:3-5) or of an entire group (Gn 35:2), is represented by new, fresh garments. This is especially true of the New Jerusalem prepared like a bride for her wedding (Is 61:10).

Once, when I was living in Nepal, our Hindu neighbor returned from a funeral, bathed at the water tap outside his house, then put on fresh clothes before reentering his home. We have seen the white garments repeatedly used in Revelation as symbols of victory and glory (3:4; 6:11; 7:14). However, they are interpreted as the righteous works of the faithful (19:8), a necessary condition for participation in the wedding feast (see Mt 22:11-14). Although the deeds are indeed their own works, still the dress is *given*; therefore, their deeds are the work of God's grace (see Eph 2:9-10). The fourth of the seven beatitudes in Revelation, presented in 19:9, further proclaims that entrance to the Lamb's wedding banquet is not mere human choice but the effect of God's call.

The seer is so overwhelmed by the revealing spirit that he wishes to worship it. However, it is only an angel (19:10). We are reminded that the temptation to idolatry may not come from someone inviting us to burn incense before an idol. It may come from something much more spiritual: to take some spiritual cause, or some "hero" who may have been the instrument of God's grace to us, then to project unreal, even divine traits upon that person.

It is a purification to discover that the "stars" or "heroes" who have enthralled us, no matter how spiritual they may appear or even be, are human after all. We find our own liberation in letting them be the creatures that they are and letting God alone be God. The messengers themselves must remember the same truth when others focus more upon their persons than upon their message and the person of Jesus. "Witness to Jesus is the spirit of prophecy" means that true prophecy can be discerned by its leading to Jesus and witnessing to him (see 1 Cor 12:1-3). Since Jesus is the Word of God in the flesh (19:13), to him alone (and not even to an angel) must divine worship be given.

THE KING OF KINGS AND LORD OF LORDS

[11]Then I saw the heavens opened, and there was a white horse; its rider was [called] "Faithful and True." He judges and wages war in righteousness. [12]His eyes were [like] a fiery flame, and on his head were many diadems. He had a name inscribed that no one knows except himself. [13]He wore a cloak that had been dipped in blood, and his name was called the Word of God. [14]The armies of heaven followed him, mounted on white horses and wearing clean

white linen. [15]Out of his mouth came a sharp sword to strike the nations. He will rule them with an iron rod, and he himself will tread out in the wine press the wine of the fury and wrath of God the almighty. [16]He has a name written on his cloak and on his thigh, "King of kings and Lord of lords."   Revelation 19:11-16

✧ ✧ ✧

Here the heavens are further opened, as they were at the baptism of Jesus (Mt 3:16; Lk 3:21). White horses were usually chosen to bear the army's leader in his victory parade. However, the seer does not tell us the rider is Jesus. Instead he calls him "faithful and true." We are thus cross-referenced to the inaugural vision of 1:5, where Jesus was called "the faithful witness" and to 3:14 where he is called "the faithful and true witness." "True" here means more than "truthful." It means reliable, loyal, committed to the covenant relationship with his people—much the same as the prologue of the fourth Gospel speaks of Jesus as the revelation of God's "grace and truth"—his faithful love—in John 1:17. The ultimate sign of that faithful love was his death on the cross.

Though the imagery is military and triumphant, it is interesting to note the weapons he bears—righteousness and his Word. *Righteousness* recalls Isaiah's description of the Messiah: "Righteousness [justice] shall be the band around his waist, and faithfulness a belt upon his hips" (Is 11:5). He comes not only as victor but as judge. "He shall judge the poor with justice, and decide aright for the land's afflicted" (Is 11:4). His blazing eyes (19:12) refer us again to the Son of Man in 1:14 and 2:18. For the first time he wears diadems (probably one on top of the other), a sign of his conquest of the diadem-headed beast (13:1). Later he is given other names, but these do not exhaust the mystery of his person: only he knows his own name (19:12). This is significant. The names given to Jesus by others and even those revealed by God never totally capture who he is, nor does the special knowledge and union with Jesus gained by the martyrs (2:17).

The cloak dipped in blood recalls the Old Testament description of the Lord's garments that were stained with the blood of the enemies he has crushed, specifically Edom (Is 63:1-5). Some scholars think John has simply transferred that image here, as part of the gruesome judgment that the Son of Man will wreak on his enemies. But it is important to remember that John rarely adopts Old Testament images without modifying them to say something new. The garment is blood-stained *before* the judgment of the nations begins. Thus other authors take the blood as Jesus' own, the blood shed on the cross. This is a strange reversal of God's way of dealing with his enemies, not crushing them but redeeming them through the blood of his own Son. Thus the blood on his cloak would be equivalent to the wounds still visible on the body of the risen Christ (Jn 20:20-29).

Other authors understand it to be the blood of the martyrs, which is now the badge of victory for Jesus. In support of this interpretation, recall that in 14:18-20 the blood shed by the martyrs was also the ingathering of the elect and the victory of the Son of Man.

His name revealed to *us* is the WORD OF GOD. Why does John select this particular title for the glorious Jesus? Is it because he relays the tradition contained in the prologue of the fourth Gospel, where the eternal WORD becomes flesh?

That is possible. There are numerous other connections in Revelation with the fourth Gospel. Perhaps, in the context of judgment, John is evoking the angel of the Exodus, who swooped down to execute judgment on the oppressing Egyptians. In Wisdom 19:15-16 that angel is called "your almighty word" who carried "the sharp sword of your inexorable decree." Here there is a reference to the WORD's sharp sword (19:15).

The armies of heaven (19:14) pick up another motif we now know well from Qumran: angels engaged in the final cosmic battle. But here too John modifies the theme. The warriors are not dressed for battle. Instead they wear the white linen for the wedding banquet (19:8). Thus they are the martyrs whose robes have been made white in the blood of the Lamb (7:14). "His blood has made their robes white, and theirs has made his red" (Caird).

The second weapon of this divine warrior is his *Word* (19:15). It is significant that the sharp sword that strikes the nations comes out of his *mouth*. If God's Word is all that he needs to create, it is also all that he needs to judge and conquer the nations. The Letter to the Hebrews celebrates its power: "Indeed, the word of God is living and effective, sharper than any two-edged sword, penetrating even between soul and spirit, joints and marrow, and able to discern reflections and thoughts of the heart" (Heb 4:12).

Here the Word refers to the preaching of the gospel itself. Like the words of the prophets, the message of the Good News is both judgment and salvation. For those who turn their backs on the light it offers, the Word can only be experienced as judgment: "The word I spoke... will condemn him on the last day" (Jn 12:48). On that day, the Messiah, as prophesied, will rule the nations with an iron rod (Ps 2:9).

Nowhere in his earthly life does Jesus use such an instrument. If the message itself is both judgment and salvation, then the iron rod must be the cross itself. It is weakness to unbelievers, but to believers it is the power of God (1 Cor 1:23-24). How paradoxically the Messiah fulfills the prophecies of old! So too with the treading out of the winepress of God's wrath (19:15). Jesus drank the cup of God's wrath for all humankind (cf. Mk 10:38-39). On the cross he treaded out the winepress in the shedding of his own blood. Eventually, however, those who shed innocent blood, whether of Jesus or the martyrs, cannot escape the effects of their own unrepented acts. Thus refusal of grace becomes judgment in the end.

On his thigh, where the sword normally hangs, there is inscribed still another name for this figure: "King of kings and Lord of lords" (19:16). The name is also emblazoned on his cloak, which is stained with his blood and the blood of the martyrs who have contributed to his victory.

FEAST OF THE BIRDS

[17]Then I saw an angel standing on the sun. He cried out [in] a loud voice to all the birds flying high overhead, "Come here. Gather for God's great feast, [18]to eat the flesh of kings, the flesh of military officers, and the flesh of warriors, the flesh of horses and of their riders, and the flesh of all, free and slave, small and great." [19]Then I saw the beast and the kings of the earth and their armies gathered to fight against the one riding the horse and against his army. [20]The beast was caught and with it the false prophet who had performed in its sight the signs by which he led astray those who had accepted the mark of the beast and those who had worshiped its image. The two were thrown alive into the fiery pool burning with sulfur. [21]The rest were killed by the sword that came out of the mouth of the one riding the horse, and all the birds gorged themselves on their flesh.   **Revelation 19:17-21**

✧ ✧ ✧

As a Jewish Christian, John could hardly conceive of the final victory of God and his people without the aid of Old Testament imagery and prophecies, especially about the triumph of Israel's God over the oppressing pagan nations. Thus John borrows the gruesome imagery of Ezekiel 39:17-22 but, as usual, freely adapts it to the victory of Christ and his faithful. The birds are obviously vultures. In 8:13 a vulture had warned of three woes, but he never actually described the third, because of John's interlocking technique in which the last of a series opens up another series (11:14-19).

Here we have what could be considered the third and final woe. It is the final defeat of the ungodly. The kings ally themselves with the Beast. Those led astray by it are slain by the sword of God's Word (19:21). The earthly powers opposed to the kingdom of God are demolished. But the Beast (the Roman persecutor) and the false prophet are given special treatment. They are caught and thrown into the pool of fire (19:20). They seem incapable of destruction, for they endure eternal torment there (20:10).

We have met the false prophet only once before (16:13). There, along with the dragon and the Beast, it was the source of demonic spirits that performed signs. In the process they assembled the kings of the earth for the final battle. Here the deception has become manifest in its defeat by the Word of God (19:21). In a sense the early church had more to fear from false prophets than from the persecutor. The false prophet seemed more likely to lead the Christian community astray *from within* through seduction and error.

Do these images suggest that John or his community is being invited to gloat in revenge? In 19:1-4 the heavenly chorus had sung its Alleluias that God had avenged the blood of his servants. "Smoke will rise from her forever and ever," and the vulture-feast (19:21) is surely a gruesome issue to the conflict. If personal vengeance were being applauded, it would not only go against Jesus' command to love one's enemies (Mt 5:43-48), but even against the admonition of Proverbs 24:17-18 cited earlier: "Rejoice not when your enemy falls, and when he stumbles, let not your heart exult, lest the Lord see it, be displeased with you, and withdraw his wrath from your enemy."

God's wrath is already dealing with the injustice. When the offended party takes wrath into his or her own hands, that person is actually interfering with the working of God's justice. "The wrath of a man does not accomplish the righteousness of God" (Jas 1:20). Though God's righteousness always works for the conversion of the sinner, he will not take away the free will he has given his spiritual creatures. This leaves the awesome possibility that the creature can decide to reject the Creator in ultimate rebellion. That can hardly be cause for rejoicing. But since injustice has been righted, the oppressed liberated, and the faithful rewarded, there is cause for rejoicing and praising the justice of God (19:1-8). At the same time there is awe and a tinge of sadness (19:21-23) that humans could be so obstinate, to their own destruction.

✧ ✧ ✧

Reflection

The image of the woman appears repeatedly in Revelation. We met her in Chapter 12 as representing both old and new Israel, mother of the messianic people who will be the object of Satan's attacks. Here we have met another woman, the whore who represents an entire value system opposed to God. Soon we will meet another woman: the bride of the Lamb, figure of the immaculate and glorious church. We are obviously being invited to choose which woman we will claim as ours, or rather, which woman will claim our love, devotion, and allegiance: the drunken harlot and idolatry, lust, and greed, or the mother-bride invested with the very holiness and glory of God.

Questions

1. Why is it necessary for John to be led into the desert to see the ugly deeds of the harlot? How does this apply to us?

   p. 195

2. Who does the Beast represent? What happens to the enemies of God?

   p. 195

3. Why did Rome fall? Could this happen to our country today?

   p 202

4. Who is the bridegroom and how is he dressed? Who is the bride, and how does she make herself ready for the wedding?

5. What does the rider who is called Faithful and True mean for my life? How should it affect my daily life?

Prayer

Lord Jesus, you are the bridegroom whose coming we await. Make us ever more ready for your coming. Reveal to us the little ways in which we listen to the siren-song of the harlot, so that, rejecting it, we may rejoice to hear the beauty of your voice. Amen.

PART THREE

✧ ✧ ✧

The Grand Finale

TEN

The Longer Future, the Final Victory, and the New Creation
(20:1–22:5)

T HE NEXT TWO CHAPTERS in Revelation raise some interesting questions: Will Christ literally reign on earth for a thousand years with the elect? What are we to make of the image of hell portrayed here? Will hell really last forever and ever? If creation is basically good, why does God create a new heaven and a new earth (Chapter 21)? Is not the notion of hell and the new creation contradictory to our conception of the goodness of God and creation? These are serious issues, and we will address them. But they should not obscure the more important message John has to give us. For that we need to listen to his revelation on his own terms.

THE LONGER FUTURE: THE MILLENNIUM

¹Then I saw an angel come down from heaven, holding in his hand the key to the abyss and a heavy chain. ²He seized the dragon, the ancient serpent, which is the

Devil or Satan, and tied it up for a thousand years ³and threw it into the abyss, which he locked over it and sealed, so that it could no longer lead the nations astray until the thousand years are completed. After this, it is to be released for a short time.

⁴Then I saw thrones; those who sat on them were entrusted with judgment. I also saw the souls of those who had been beheaded for their witness to Jesus and for the word of God, and who had not worshiped the beast or its image nor had accepted its mark on their foreheads or hands. They came to life and they reigned with Christ for a thousand years. ⁵The rest of the dead did not come to life until the thousand years were over. This is the first resurrection. ⁶Blessed and holy is the one who shares in the first resurrection. The second death has no power over these; they will be priests of God and of Christ, and they will reign with him for [the] thousand years.

Revelation 20:1-6

✧ ✧ ✧

This passage has given rise to Millenarianism (or *Chiliasm,* from the Greek word for one thousand). It maintains that Christ will return to the earth in order to establish an earthly kingdom that will last for one thousand years (understood literally). At his coming the martyrs and all the faithful will come to life in a first resurrection. For one thousand years they will share his royal priesthood in a messianic kingdom on earth. Toward the end of that time and after a bitter struggle, Satan will be defeated by Christ in the last judgment. Sinners will then rise from the grave to be plunged into the pool of fire (the "second death"). Meanwhile the elect enter the eternal happiness of heaven.

Today this teaching is held by Seventh Day Adventists, the Southern Baptist Convention, Second Adventists, Primitive

Baptists, Mormons, and Jehovah's Witnesses. In a different form, Joachim of Fiore (A.D. 1201) predicted that there would be a thousand-year age of the Holy Spirit beginning in A.D. 1260. The Millennarist idea even inspired the Peasants' War of 1525, led by Thomas Münzer. He held that only the poor would be worthy of the millennium; the means he proclaimed to establish the millennium was to overthrow and annihilate the wealthy.

All of these interpretations are based on a literal understanding of this passage and of the thousand years. But Augustine, already aware that the literal understanding of the thousand-year earthly reign is not supported by any other New Testament text, proposed that one thousand years are to be taken symbolically—for the whole history of the church (both in heaven and on earth), from Christ's resurrection until his second coming. The "first resurrection" refers to the new life given by Christ to the sinner in faith and baptism (described in Rom 6:1-8 as a dying and rising with Christ). This interpretation is still current in many circles, Catholic and Protestant. It appears in the notes of the New American Bible (Revised New Testament).

The symbolic meaning of one thousand years is more consistent with the symbolism of numbers in Revelation. John's literary camera follows an angel from heaven to earth (20:1). The dragon which the angel encounters was mentioned in Chapter 12; there he had gone off to make war on the woman's other children (the Christians, 12:17). The beasts, which were his instruments, have already been thrown into the fiery pit (19:20). The dragon (the ancient serpent, the devil, Satan) is still roaming about. Now the angel ties him up and throws him into the abyss for one thousand years (20:2-3). Virtually all the numbers elsewhere in Revelation are symbolic, therefore it would be rash to take the number one thousand here mathematically. It is symbolic of a *long period of time*. This era will be relatively free from Satan's seductive activity. At the end of it the dragon will be released for a short time. Our camera here is fixed on the earthly stage.

Is the scene beginning with 20:4 also on earth? Or are we again viewing the heavenly counterpart?

Whenever John sees thrones, and he does so forty-seven times in Revelation, it is always in heaven—the only exception being the thrones of Satan (2:13) or the Beast (13:2; 16:10). Here John also sees the souls of the martyrs (20:4). The expression is almost identical with 6:9, where the souls of the martyrs are under the heavenly altar. The victors must be the same as those who stand on the heavenly sea of glass in 15:1-2, and those to whom the Son of Man promises a share in his heavenly throne (3:21).

These references indicate that John has switched us back to the heavenly scene, to tell us what is going on there during the one thousand years that Satan is bound below. This switching technique has been used repeatedly in Revelation. The martyrs are reigning with Christ in heaven, but their reign, like that of Christ, is also on earth. Their sacrifice, like that of Christ, has brought about the binding of Satan.

All of the redeemed had been promised an earthly rule in 5:10. The reign promised here is to those "beheaded for their witness to Jesus" (20:4)—the martyrs. They alone "come to life" in a first resurrection and reign with Christ for the one thousand years (20:4-5). There is no indication that they are physically present on earth any more than Christ is. In keeping with John's two-stage drama, they reign with Christ in heaven, while the effects of their sacrifice are felt on earth. In this interpretation, the martyrs have already experienced the resurrection in a way that the rest of the dead have not yet.

The fifth of the seven beatitudes in Revelation appears in 20:6. It proclaims the bliss of the martyrs. They have already escaped the "second death"—damnation. Perhaps this is the conclusion of the judgment we were led to expect when we first saw the thrones—they were thrones for judgment

(20:4). We were not told who sat on these thrones. In the synoptic tradition it would be the twelve apostles (Mt 19:12; Lk 22:29-30). But according to Revelation, the victorious martyrs also share Christ's throne. Perhaps they also share in his judging activity. They certainly share in Christ's priesthood, offering their shed blood with his as sacrifice and intercession (cf. Heb 9:12-14).

If we understand the one thousand years as John's view of the church's history (from the period of the martyrs until the final day of the Lord), then one thing is clear. The effects of Jesus' death and resurrection, as well as the death and resurrection of the martyrs with him, are manifested on earth by the beneficent influence of the church restraining the power of Satan. It is a real reigning on earth (cf. 1 Cor 15:25). It is not the final reign, which will be the new heaven and the new earth soon to be described in Chapters 21 and 22.

SATAN'S FINAL DEFEAT

[7]When the thousand years are completed, Satan will be released from his prison. [8]He will go out to deceive the nations at the four corners of the earth, Gog and Magog, to gather them for battle; their number is like the sand of the sea. [9]They invaded the breadth of the earth and surrounded the camp of the holy ones and the beloved city. But fire came down from heaven and consumed them. [10]The Devil who had led them astray was thrown into the pool of fire and sulfur, where the beast and the false prophet were. There they will be tormented day and night forever and ever.   **Revelation 20:7-10**

❖ ❖ ❖

In keeping with other New Testament understandings of the final period (before the very end of world history as we know it), the restraining of Satan is removed. There is a final but brief outbreak of consummate evil (see 2 Thes 2:6-10), again in the form of deception and seduction (20:8). John evokes the "Gog and Magog" imagery from Ezekiel 38-39. There the prophet also describes the final battle of God against the forces of evil. Magog was listed as one of the northern nations in Genesis 10:2.

The Jewish historian Josephus, a contemporary of John, said the Magogites are the ones the Greeks call Scythians (*Ant.* 1:6, 1). But for Ezekiel the term already has become symbolic for all the enemies of God's people. The Jewish Talmud says "Gog and Magog" are the nations that rebel against God's Messiah in Psalm 2. That seems to be the meaning here—not the peoples of the nations (for many of them are now in the church) but the political forces that have oppressed the church and tried to destroy the gospel of Jesus Christ.

The "camp of the holy ones" and the beautiful name "beloved city" (20:9) stand for the church. Perhaps surrounding the city was suggested by the Romans' invasion of Jerusalem before they destroyed it in A.D. 70. Later, in the creation of the new heaven and the new earth, the holy city descends from heaven (21:10). Here it is the church embattled on earth.

A final heavenly intervention saves the church, destroying the political powers. The devil is thrown into the fiery abyss to join the Beast and the false prophet (20:10). The finality of this defeat is emphasized by the climactic "day and night, forever and ever."

The struggle (which began in Chapter 12) between the dragon and the people of God is brought to a conclusion in Chapters 19 and 20, by reversing the protagonists' order of appearance. In Chapter 12:3 the dragon appeared, then the faithful (12:17), then the beasts (13:1, 11). The beasts are first defeated (19:20), then the faithful martyrs rise and reign (20:4-6); finally the dragon is defeated (20:10).

THE FINAL JUDGMENT

[11]Next I saw a large white throne and the one who was sitting on it. The earth and the sky fled from his presence and there was no place for them. [12]I saw the dead, the great and the lowly, standing before the throne, and scrolls were opened. Then another scroll was opened, the book of life. The dead were judged according to their deeds, by what was written in the scrolls. [13]The sea gave up its dead; then Death and Hades gave up their dead. All the dead were judged according to their deeds. [14]Then Death and Hades were thrown into the pool of fire. (This pool of fire is the second death.) [15]Anyone whose name was not found written in the book of life was thrown into the pool of fire.   **Revelation 20:11-15**

❖ ❖ ❖

The great white throne is obviously the throne of God. The earth and the sky not only disappear—they *flee* from the divine presence as unworthy. "There was no place for them" is not simply redundance. It is an expression taken from Daniel's description of Nebuchadnezzar's dream (Dn 2:35). The statue, a symbol of earthly kingdoms, was swept away by the kingdom of God "without leaving a trace" (20:11). John has already used this term in 12:8 to describe Satan's banishment from heaven.

The earth and sky then must stand, not for the beautiful creation that once came from God's hand nor even for their transitory nature, but for the religio-political order of the cosmos opposed to his purpose. It is the chaotic world constructed by human sinfulness and oppressive human structures, the creation marred from primeval times by man's rebellion against God (Gn 3) and his violence against his fellowman (Gn 4). It is abetted by all the sin of the ages that has turned creation away from its original purpose.

The judgment of all the dead now takes place, using the classic imagery of the scrolls on which the good and evil deeds of each person are recorded (20:12). The dead come from three places: the sea, death itself, and the netherworld (20:13). Actually death and the netherworld are the same. The sea is mentioned separately (20:13); those who died there were unable to be covered by the earth in proper burial and unable to enter hades (the netherworld which was often conceived as a waiting place for the resurrection). Each person is judged according to his or her deeds.

Then death itself (and its home, hades) is destroyed (20:14): "The last enemy to be destroyed is death... 'Death is swallowed up in victory. Where, O death, is your victory? Where, O death, is your sting?'" (1 Cor 15:26, 54-55). The pool of fire, the second death, is eternal punishment. Into the pool go those whose names were not written in the book of life (20:15). This is not predestinationism—where God would arbitrarily choose some for salvation and some for damnation. Instead, as the text itself has made explicit, it is the deeds of men and women that are written down. The judgment is based on these.

We now begin the final climactic section. In this the theme is the new heaven, the new earth, and the heavenly city of God, the New Jerusalem. Nine elements of the old order disappear: the sea (21:1), tears, death, mourning, wailing, pain (21:4), the unclean (21:27), all that is under God's curse (22:3), and night (22:5). Of these, the sea and the night symbolized in Jewish tradition the primeval chaos out of which God created. There was always in them a reminder of that earlier chaos which could return and engulf human life (as happened in the time of the flood and the darkness at the death of Jesus). The new creation, therefore, does not necessarily involve the physical destruction of the universe. It does imply a total remaking of it according to God's perfect blueprint.

THE NEW HEAVEN AND THE NEW EARTH

[1]Then I saw a new heaven and a new earth. The former heaven and the former earth had passed away, and the sea was no more. [2]I also saw the holy city, a new Jerusalem, coming down out of heaven from God, prepared as a bride adorned for her husband. [3]I heard a loud voice from the throne saying, "Behold, God's dwelling is with the human race. He will dwell with them and they will be his people and God himself will always be with them [as their God]. [4]He will wipe every tear from their eyes, and there shall be no more death or mourning, wailing or pain, [for] the old order has passed away."

[5]The one who sat on the throne said, "Behold, I make all things new." Then he said, "Write these words down, for they are trustworthy and true." [6]He said to me, "They are accomplished. I [am] the Alpha and the Omega, the beginning and the end. To the thirsty I will give a gift from the spring of life-giving water. [7]The victor will inherit these gifts, and I shall be his God, and he will be my son. [8]But as for cowards, the unfaithful, the depraved, murderers, the unchaste, sorcerers, idol-worshipers, and deceivers of every sort, their lot is in the burning pool of fire and sulfur, which is the second death."   **Revelation 21:1-8**

❖ ❖ ❖

This is really a prologue introducing the content that will be developed further in the final chapters (21:9-22:5). That there should be a new earth we can easily understand, but how can there be a new heaven? Is not heaven the place of God's dwelling, the place of perfection?

Throughout Revelation John has presented the struggle on earth as having its counterpart in the heavenly realm: the place of the heavenly combat between Satan and his angels, the place from which they are cast out (12:7-9). It is the place also of the heavenly sea which is in front of the throne, representing God's unfinished agenda—the trouble which he permits to take place on earth. It becomes the footstool of the victorious martyrs (15:2).

Now all this has passed and perfect peace reigns in the new heaven and new earth. The sea (remnant and reminder of the primeval chaos) was the turf of the dragon (12:18), the home of the Beast (13:1), and the throne of the harlot (17:1). Charged with memories of the Exodus from Egypt, the sea was the chaos through which the martyrs had to pass. Since John makes no distinction here between the earthly sea and heavenly sea of 4:6, we assume both of them disappear. This confirms our interpretation of the heavenly sea as the earthly sea's counterpart.

Combining images, John sees the heavenly city as a bride dressed for her wedding (21:2; Is 61:10). Why does the holy city come down from heaven? Would it not be sufficient for the city to remain in heaven and the victorious people to be taken up there?

No. John is convinced that the new creation is a transformation of both earth and heaven. Even more, it is the wedding of heaven and earth. In the Lord's Prayer, Christians have prayed that "thy kingdom come," meaning that God's will be done *on earth* as it is in heaven. Revelation is not escapist theology. It takes seriously the aim and purpose of the first creation. While God intervenes in history he despises nothing of what he has made (Wis 11:24). He crowns it at the end by bringing heaven and earth together. This is the sense of 21:3—it is God's dwelling with the human race. The Greek word for dwelling is *skene*. It translates the Hebrew *mishkan* meaning tent and evokes the tent in which the Lord dwelt among his people in the desert. It was later understood to be the temple. Since there will be no temple in the New Jerusalem, the meaning must be simply his presence. "They will be his people" recalls the promise made in the first covenant: "I will set my dwelling among you.... Ever present in your midst, I will be your God, and you will be my people" (Lv 26:11-12; cf. Jer 7:23; 11:4; Hos 1:9).

There will be no suffering—physical, emotional, or spiritual there (21:4). John borrows some of his imagery from the vision of the messianic banquet (Is 25:6-8). The "old order" (or in some translations, "the former world") is not simply the past, for God was at work already in the lives of the martyrs. It is the disordered world of sin and chaos. It is not just "a new thing" God is doing, like the return from exile in Isaiah 43:19. He is making *all* things new (21:5): a new creation.

Writing the words down is equivalent to an assurance that, in God's determination, they have already been fulfilled. He is the Alpha and the Omega (the first and last letters of the Greek alphabet), the beginning and the end (21:6). As God is the beginning of all creation and of its history, so he is its end.

Perhaps now we can see why John has often brought us to the end, only to start us all over again. The *end* is not a thing or an event but a person. The neuter form *eschaton* (last) never appears in the New Testament. There is only the *eschatos* (masculine singular)—the person who *is* the end. Being both beginning and end does not mean that he is absent from the middle. John is no deist. Throughout Revelation we have seen God intervening in historical events. But to be in touch with the end of everything even in the present, all we need do is to be in touch with him who is the end. That may mean nothing more than thirsting for him.

The promise made here echoes those made in each of the letters to the churches (Chapters 2-3). Here it is the image of the living water Jesus used in the fourth Gospel to describe the Spirit he would give (Jn 4:10; 7:37). In the other New Testament literature the Spirit is given in the present. John sees it as a gift of the consummation, just as it is the gift of sonship (21:7, echoing 2 Sm 7:14, the promise made to the house of David).

There is no contradiction in the two views. Even we who receive the spirit and the sonship, here and now (Gal 4:4-7; Rom 8:14-17), are promised to discover fully what it means in eternity (1 Jn 3:2). This is the essence of the cosmic fulfillment. All the rest is simply the resonance of this central truth that God is Father and that we are his beloved children in Jesus. The *end* is knowing his embrace: "Creation awaits with eager expectation the revelation of the children of God" (Rom 8:19).

On the other hand, among those destined to the pool of fire and the second death (20:8) are those listed first, the cowards. John doubtless means those who under persecution became apostates. Thus John offers a stern reminder to those who are still faced with a choice.

THE HOLY CITY: NEW JERUSALEM

[9]One of the seven angels who held the seven bowls filled with the seven last plagues came and said to me, "Come here. I will show you the bride, the wife of the Lamb." [10]He took me in spirit to a great, high mountain and showed me the holy city Jerusalem coming down out of heaven from God. [11]It gleamed with the splendor of God. Its radiance was like that of a precious stone, like jasper, clear as crystal. [12]It had a massive, high wall, with

twelve gates where twelve angels were stationed and on which names were inscribed, [the names] of the twelve tribes of the Israelites. [13]There were three gates facing east, three north, three south, and three west. [14]The wall of the city had twelve courses of stones as its foundation, on which were inscribed the twelve names of the twelve apostles of the Lamb.

[15]The one who spoke to me held a gold measuring rod to measure the city, its gates, and its wall. [16]The city was square, its length the same as [also] its width. He measured the city with the rod and found it fifteen hundred miles in length and width and height. [17]He also measured its wall: one hundred and forty-four cubits according to the standard unit of measurement the angel used. [18]The wall was constructed of jasper, while the city was pure gold, clear as glass. [19]The foundations of the city wall were decorated with every precious stone; the first course of stones was jasper, the second sapphire, the third chalcedony, the fourth emerald, the fifth sardonyx, the sixth carnelian, the seventh chrysolite, the eighth beryl, the ninth topaz, the tenth chrysoprase, the eleventh hyacinth, and the twelfth amethyst. [21]The twelve gates were twelve pearls, each of the gates made from a single pearl; and the street of the city was of pure gold, transparent as glass.

[22]I saw no temple in the city, for its temple is the Lord God almighty and the Lamb. [23]The city had no need of sun or moon to shine on it, for the glory of God gave it light, and its lamp was the Lamb. [24]The nations will walk by its light, and to it the kings of the earth will bring their treasure. [25]During the day its gates will never be shut, and there will be no night there. [26]The treasure and wealth of the nations will be brought there, [27]but nothing unclean will enter it, nor any[one] who does abominable things or tells lies. Only those will enter whose names are written in the Lamb's book of life.   **Revelation 21:9-27**

❖ ❖ ❖

It is strange that the glorious vision of the New Jerusalem is shown to John by one of the angels of the plagues (20:9). It was not so strange when the same angel showed him the great harlot, Babylon (in 17:1). No doubt using the same messenger for both, John wants to draw a contrast between the two women: the earthly Rome and the heavenly Jerusalem. More importantly, perhaps, John wants his readers not to forget that the descent of the heavenly city has been won by the martyrs. It is related to the preceding struggle.

Again, the city is bride and wife of the Lamb. Love, covenant bonding, sacrifice—all are evoked by this most powerful image of the church in its consummate stage. The mountain (21:10) is the site not of the viewer but of the city itself, as Ezekiel saw (40:2). Adapting an ancient myth about a mountain in the far north which reached the heavens and was the home of the gods (perhaps the Himalayas?), Ezekiel identifies this "mountain of God" with "Eden, the garden of God" (Ez 28:12-16). It is the same passage from which John draws his list of precious stones. Psalm 48:2 states that this mountain is really Zion, the mount on which Jerusalem is built (cf. also Is 2:2; Mi 4:1).

At the end of this development, John applies the image to the New Jerusalem, the place where God and humanity meet. It is significant that, although John later describes heaven as seeing God face to face (see 22:4), he does not think of this in an individual sense (as if they were attending an opera and each looking on God through binoculars, with no concern about the person next to them). Heaven is a fellowship, a city, a corporate body.

The descent of this city from heaven must not be thought of in a geographical sense, nor even as a chronological moment. This is a theological statement. At all times, in whatever the circumstances, the city of God comes from heaven—it is not built by humans. This is simply a graphic way of explaining the divine origin of the city and its transcendent goal. However, John is obviously here thinking of its glorious consummation, for it gleams with the splendor of God (21:11). John is inspired by Ezekiel's vision of the New Jerusalem (Ez 48:30-35). Typically he adapts it, making the gates entrances for the nations (21:24, 28) instead of exits, and changing the order of listing the gates (east, north, south, west; see 21:13). This is possibly to avoid a zodiacal interpretation. He adds foundation stones which are the historical apostles (21:14).

Thus the New Jerusalem is made of Jews and gentiles. It is founded upon the twelve apostles (cf. Eph 2:20). Here it is evident that the descriptions of this city are symbolic: the city is a perfect cube, with astronomical proportions—1,500 miles each dimension—indicating the universality of this city (21:15-16). The wall is measured by cubits, but though the cubit is the length of a human forearm, the measuring rod here is angelic. Who knows what an angelic cubit is (21:17)? Though made of gold, the city and its streets are also transparent (21:18, 21), at once most precious and pure. Human metaphors collapse in their attempts to describe the grandeur of this city!

Finally, the decorative stones (21:19-21) are the stones which adorned the high priest's robe (Ex 28:17-21; 39:10-14). According to Wisdom 18:24 they had a cosmic significance: "On his full-length robe was the whole world." R.H. Charles compiles evidence from Egyptian and Arabic monuments showing the twelve stones are symbols of the zodiac. The order is from amethyst (Ram) to jasper (Pisces), the actual path of the sun through the zodiac. John retains the cosmic symbolism but he has deliberately reversed the order so that we do not associate it with astrology.

The temple and other physical symbols of God's presence among his people on earth now give way to reality and immediacy: "At present we see indistinctly, but then face to face" (1 Cor 13:12). In ancient Jewish thought, we would expect to find a heavenly temple, a counterpart of the earthly one. But there is none (21:22).

The realm of the sacred extends to the entire city. All is holy, imbued with the presence of God. There is no need for physical lights, for God is its light and the Lamb its lamp (21:23)—an incredible theological image for the Son as mediator of the splendor of the Father (Heb 1:3).

After all the destructive imagery in the preceding chapters, it may be a surprise to see the nations and even their kings appearing here, bringing their treasures into the holy city (21:24)! It is obvious, then, that Revelation does not envision the complete destruction of the nations nor their kings as such but only the transformation that is necessary for them to enter the kingdom of God, fulfilling the prophecies of old (Is 60:1-11).

Since there is no night, there is no need to close the city gates (21:25; Is 60:11). There are no locks on the doors of heaven! All that is created good has been redeemed, will be found in the city, but nothing impure, obscene or false, will be found there. On the book of life, see above, 20:12-15.

THE HEART OF HEAVEN

[1]Then the angel showed me the river of life-giving water, sparkling like crystal, flowing from the throne of God and of the Lamb [2]down the middle of its street. On either side of the river grew the tree of life that produces fruit twelve times a year, once each month; the leaves of the trees serve as medicine for the nations. [3]Nothing accursed will be found there anymore. The throne of God and of the Lamb will be in it, and his servants will worship him. [4]They will look upon his face, and his

name will be on their foreheads. [5]Night will be no more, nor will they need light for lamp or sun, for the Lord God shall give them light, and they shall reign forever and ever.   Revelation 22:1-5

❖ ❖ ❖

In the Old Testament, the life of God was compared to light; it was also compared with water. Consequently John cannot think of the consummation of divine life without the image of living water. He draws on Ezekiel's vision of the New Jerusalem: the great river flowed from the new temple out to the Dead Sea, which became fresh with fish. Along its bank grew trees bearing fruit each month with healing in their leaves (Ez 47:1-12). John typically transforms this imagery. The river becomes the river of Eden: it is paradise regained. The water is life-giving water (the "water of life" or the "living water" of the Johannine tradition). The trees become the one tree of life (22:2). Although this makes the image of the single tree growing on both sides of the river a bit clumsy, he does so to stress in another way that paradise is regained (Gn 2:9-10). No longer is there a flaming sword barring access to the tree of immortality. The river does not flow toward the Arabah but down the middle of each street (see Ps 46:5). The medicinal leaves of the trees become healing leaves for the *nations.*

The source of the river is no longer the temple (since there is no temple), but the throne of God and of the Lamb. This image in 22:1, with the river of life flowing from God and the Lamb, would become an important one in the later church as it struggled to more clearly define the doctrine of the Trinity. The Greek word for *flowing from* would be used to describe the Holy Spirit proceeding from the Father and Son.

In the fourth Gospel Jesus speaks of the Holy Spirit as liv-

ing water (Jn 4:10; 7:37-38). He says that the Spirit proceeds from the Father (Jn 15:26) or will be sent by the
Father (Jn 14:16, 26) in Jesus' name (Jn 14:26). Paul
describes Jesus as the spiritual rock from which the water of
the Spirit flows (1 Cor 10:4).

The author of Revelation captures all this in the magnificent image of the river of life flowing from God and the
Lamb. There are not two thrones but one: the Father and
the Son share one power, one authority, one reign. Together
they are one source of life.

The service given by the saints is that of worship (22:3).
The direct vision of God and the Lamb (see 1 Cor 13:12)
will be confirmed by the name of the Lamb inscribed on the
forehead of each, emphasizing the consummation of
covenant union (22:4). The thought is repeated in 22:23-25,
then concludes with a drum roll: "They shall reign forever
and ever"—the glorious counterpart to the doom of the
devil, the Beast, and the false prophet (22:10).

At this point the reader should consider consulting the
timeline on pages 12-13.

The long section we have been examining shows us that
more is at issue here than the questions we raised at the
beginning. Yes, we now know what Christ's thousand-year
reign with the martyrs means. We know that the old earth
and sea and sky that pass away are the despotic powers that
have ruled them and not God's good creation. We know that
the new creation is nothing less than God's plan for the universe and history brought to its final consummation. And
from all that we have said throughout the commentary, we
know that if hell is eternal it is so only for those whose will is
fixed in unchangeable hatred of God and refusal to surrender
to his rule of love.

But these questions are not the heart of this beautiful climax
to the Book of Revelation. John has mustered all his biblical
imagination to paint for us the magnificence of the final goal,

the heavenly Jerusalem. It is a life of supreme happiness and joy, of eternal bonding as citizens of a city which is also the family household of God, where all know what it is to be his children. It is a life fed by the inexhaustible fountain of the Blessed Trinity. The fears that lead us on earth to lock our doors, the sorrows that bring tears, and death that muffles hope—all are banished. All is light. The deep wells of the unknown, even within ourselves, are now forgotten because we are face to face with the infinite Unknown who is known and yet known to be beyond knowledge. The arms of our love embrace God without enclosing him, while he embraces us totally and draws us ever deeper into his infinite love.

✧ ✧ ✧

Reflection

When the psalmist looked at the heavens, he said, "When I behold your heavens, the work of your fingers, the moon and the stars which you set in place—what am I that you should even give me a thought, a mere human being that you should care for me?" (Ps 8:5, my translation). If creation so impressed the psalmist, what would we say when looking upon the face of the Creator himself, knowing that he is also our Father—indeed, One who has drawn us into his own life of infinite beauty and love?

The consummation is also described as a kingdom, where we shall reign forever and ever. God is not promising to fill our human lust for power and domination. What he is promising is that we will share in his reign, which is a reign of pure love and gift. It is a rule in which we can already begin to share in this life. The key is allowing his love to rule our hearts and, through prayer and witness, seeking to extend that love to the world.

Questions

1. What does the thousand-year reign mean in heaven and on earth?

    p. 219

2. What will the new heaven be like? Will we be part of it?

    p. 225 - 226

3. Why does the holy city come down from heaven? What will it be like?

    p. 226 - p 228   p 230

4. How do we see a figure of the Father, Son, and Holy Spirit in the holy city?

5. How can I apply this to my life? Is it a source of encouragement?

Prayer

Holy Lamb of God, gift of the Father and innocent victim slain for our sins, lead me to your throne, bathe me in the river of your Holy Spirit, that I may be worthy to share your own intimate life. With Mary and all the saints and angels, may I have the unspeakable joy of seeing you, my infinite lover, face to face. Amen.

ELEVEN

The Final Message and Our Response
(22:6–22:21)

T HE DRAMA IS ENDED. Now the listener is invited to consider the whole book which he or she has heard. (Revelation 22:18 makes clear that the idea of a private reader of a book is a modern concept foreign to the books of the New Testament, which were written for public reading.) The listener is brought back to Jesus, the glorious Son of Man, with whom the book opened. We are called to consider soberly the prophetic messages of Jesus to the church, to receive the wisdom of life from him who is the Alpha and the Omega, the First and the Last. With expectant joy we are invited to receive the waters of life from him who alone can fill our hunger and thirst.

THE EPILOGUE

> 6And he said to me, "These words are trustworthy and true, and the Lord, the God of prophetic spirits, sent his angel to show his servants what must happen soon.

⁷"Behold, I am coming soon." Blessed is the one who keeps the prophetic message of this book.

⁸It is I, John, who heard and saw these things, and when I heard and saw them I fell down to worship at the feet of the angel who showed them to me. ⁹But he said to me, "Don't! I am a fellow servant of yours and of your brothers the prophets and of those who keep the message of this book. Worship God."

¹⁰Then he said to me, "Do not seal up the prophetic words of this book, for the appointed time is near. ¹¹Let the wicked still act wickedly, and the filthy still be filthy. The righteous must still do right, and the holy still be holy."

¹²"Behold, I am coming soon. I bring with me the recompense I will give to each according to his deeds. ¹³I am the Alpha and the Omega, the first and the last, the beginning and the end."

¹⁴Blessed are they who wash their robes so as to have the right to the tree of life and enter the city through its gates. ¹⁵Outside are the dogs, the sorcerers, the unchaste, the murderers, the idol-worshipers, and all who love and practice deceit.

¹⁶"I, Jesus, sent my angel to give you this testimony for the churches. I am the root and offspring of David, the bright morning star."

¹⁷The Spirit and the bride say, "Come." Let the hearer say, "Come." Let the one who thirsts come forward, and the one who wants it receive the gift of life-giving water.

¹⁸I warn everyone who hears the prophetic words in this book: if anyone adds to them, God will add to him the plagues described in this book, ¹⁹and if anyone takes away from the words in this prophetic book, God will take away his share in the tree of life and in the holy city described in this book.

²⁰The one who gives this testimony says, "Yes, I am coming soon." Amen! Come, Lord Jesus! *[handwritten: 3rd terme]*
²¹The grace of the Lord Jesus be with all. Revelation 22:6-21

[handwritten: Cor 16:32]

❖ ❖ ❖

After the magnificent vision, we are now brought back to the prophetic experience which began the Book of Revelation. Notice the many parallels with the prologue and the inaugural vision in Chapter 1.

Verse 22:6 acts as a great seal stamped upon the whole book. The words are "faithful and true" because they come from him who is faithful and true (3:14; 19:11). The office of prophet was a common one in the early church (cf. Eph 2:20). Here each prophet is moved by a particular spirit but all coming from the one God. It is a peculiarity of Revelation that these spirits are either angels or the Holy Spirit in his various charismatic manifestations (see George Montague, *The Holy Spirit: Growth of a Biblical Tradition*, 321-332). Here the "servants" to whom these things are shown are all Christians, especially those exposed to the coming great tribulation—the things "that must happen soon." Thus we see that John's immediate concern is to strengthen the faithful for the persecution about to break out.

The speaker in 22:7 is no longer the angel but Jesus, who reaffirms that he is coming soon in judgment and reward (2:16; 3:11). The sixth beatitude of Revelation echoes the first: it blesses both the reader and the hearer of the book (1:3). Now having heard, only the one who lives this message will be blessed. The passage 22:8-9 repeats the incident of 19:10, with two additional points of information: 1) John belongs to a brotherhood of prophets; and 2) the revealing angel is no greater than the Christian who keeps the message he reveals.

Daniel had been told to "keep secret the message and seal the book until the end time" (8:26; 10:14; 12:4-9). Enoch was told that what he saw was not "for this generation, but for a distant one yet to come" (1 Enoch 1:2). Those authors were putting their works under the pen name of a great figure from the past. This is how they explained the intervening time before the time at which they were writing.

But John writes in his own name. Leaving the book unsealed indicates that the events are about to happen (22:10). In biblical thought, prophetic words not only describe the future—they in some way create or launch it, for history could not move forward without God's permission. The wicked must be allowed to proceed with their freely chosen deeds. The righteous and the holy must also be given the chance to show their true colors, with the warning that they not be seduced into following the wicked if these do not convert (22:11; cf. Ps 73:3). Let the drama, of which this book is the script, proceed!

After the Lord again promises his imminent return with judgment and reward (22:12), once more he uses his titles of the Beginning and the End. This signals that as we reach the end of the book, we should meet him whom we met at the beginning (22:13). These titles used for God in Isaiah 41:4; 44:6; 48:12 (and Rv 1:8; 21:6) are also used for Christ as in 1:17 and 2:8, indicating his divine status.

The seventh and last beatitude of Revelation (22:14) echoes 7:14, where the victors enter heaven because they have washed their robes and made them white in the blood of the Lamb. Though the blessing is available to all Christians, John probably has particularly in mind those who, faced with martyrdom, freely choose it in fidelity to Christ. Those outside are those who remain committed to the idols and the lifestyle of the harlot: Rome. The "you" in 22:16 is plural; the message is being addressed to all Christians, but particularly to the prophets who are expected to lead the church in its witness to Jesus. He is the root and offspring of David (the Messiah promised in Is 11:1, 10 and introduced in the vision of the Lamb in Rv 5:5). He is also the Morning Star. The prophet Balaam had seen a star rising out of Jacob, a symbol of a great leader from Israel (Nm 24:17), whom the early Christian writers took to mean the Messiah. Here the star is bright; it is the morning star. Jesus announces the end of all night (21:25; 22:5) and the dawning of that eternal light which will forever illumine the city of God.

The Spirit (22:17) is the Holy Spirit who inspires the prophets. The bride is the heavenly Jerusalem. Their "come" can be thought as addressed to Jesus, inviting him to come as he has promised. The rest of the passage, however, suggests that this "come" is addressed to the church on earth. This invites the faithful to enter the holy city in the company of the martyrs who have preceded them. The hearer (the member of the liturgical assembly) answers, "come," begging Jesus to come and hoping to meet him halfway. The hearer is now walking forward at the invitation of the Spirit to meet the Lord in the community of the saints.

The liturgical setting of these lines is unmistakable. Perhaps we have here a fragment of a hymn accompanying the celebration of baptism. The water of the sacrament was, in its turn, a symbol of the gift of the Spirit (the "life-giving water"). But this text may also reflect a eucharistic celebration: the first "come" being an invitation to communion, the second the faithful's response. From the earliest times the church considered the Eucharist to be an anticipation, a celebration, a sign, of the Lord's coming—the best thing it could do "until he comes" (1 Cor 11:26).

After using the conventional adjuration or curse with which ancient authors, especially of those sacred books, sealed their work (22:18-19), John lets Jesus show that he is the real author of the book. The play on the word "come" brings the book to its finish (22:20). The liturgical assembly has just cried "come" (22:17). Now Jesus, whose revelation they have heard, responds for the third time with his guarantee: "Yes, I am coming soon!" To which the assembly again cries: "We believe it is so! Come, Lord Jesus!"

It would go completely against the thrust of Revelation to interpret this as a prayer to escape the forthcoming trial. Elsewhere John gives no glimmer of hope that such an escape is possible. The church of Revelation is in Gethsemane with Jesus. Unlike the disciples who fell asleep, the rest of the church is awake (3:2-3; 16:15) and waiting for him to come in his passion, a necessary prelude to his return in glory. It is a church that prays daily, "Your kingdom come... and let us not fall in the final testing." In the liturgical celebration of Jesus' death and resurrection, the church asks to persevere through the upcoming tribulation to hasten the victorious coming of her Spouse.

Though a prophecy, the Book of Revelation is rolled in the form of a letter, of which the last verse (22:21) is the final greeting.

OUR RESPONSE TO REVELATION

Understanding Apocalyptic Time. It has been a classical position that the Greek notion of time was cyclical, while the biblical notion was linear. The Greeks thought of time repeating itself in the same rhythm of the seasons of nature. There was change, but more in the sense of rotation than of any new breakthrough into the uncharted future. "Time seems to be a circle," stated Aristotle.

The biblical writers, on the other hand, knew of a God of history, a God who spoke and acted in events. In this view time emerges more as a line plotted out by the successive interventions of the Lord. This gives rise to a future hope, eschatology, and messianism.

This contrast is an oversimplification. For the Israelites also celebrated the seasons in annual festivals tied to the agricultural year:

1. the Feast of the Unleavened Bread celebrating the barley harvest;
2. the Feast of Weeks celebrating the wheat harvest;
3. the Feast of Tabernacles celebrating the vintage;
4. the New Year's festival.

These festivals were also tied to the major events of Israel's history—the Exodus from Egypt, the giving of the Law on Mount Sinai, and the sojourn in the desert. So a more accurate model for biblical time is the spiral: a movement forward or upward, but at the same time a reliving of the sacred moments of the past, the "remembering" that took place. The temple priesthood fostered the cyclic movement. The prophets, on the other hand, pushed toward the future. That future was rooted in the covenant union that was more fundamental than any of its celebrations.

What about the Book of Revelation? It claims to be prophecy, so it should not be a surprise that Revelation is preoccupied with the future. But how does it treat the future?

In cyclic patterns! Each of the cycles, with the exception of the last, seems to be treating the same mystery of the future from different points of view. The cycles are interlocked, for the last part of the first three series opens up the next series. Moreover, many of the future scenes are replays of Old Testament scenes, although at a different level. This is especially true in the series of bowls, which pick up the Egyptian plagues; but the practice is evident elsewhere. The linear model we have drawn must not be overly pressed. We must especially avoid a rigid chronological timeline. As we have repeatedly stressed, John's numbers are symbolic: three and a half years means a short time, a thousand years a long time—and so on.

This alerts us to a dimension of time that is foreign to our ordinary way of thinking. There is *chronological time,* which is simply the flat succession of events without one event being more important than another. A security video camera does this in a store, without making a judgment on anything it records.

Then there is *kairotic* time (time in the sense of "moment"), an opportunity, or some happening that is significant for history. In our example, the camera catches a shoplifter—but only because an intelligence outside the camera interprets the significance of that particular customer's action. Biblical history is made of these *kairotic* moments. Since they are interpreted by divine revelation to be God's actions, something of his overall purposes can be discerned from looking at any one of them.

Thus *kairotic* time often becomes *proleptic* time: one event anticipates, or predicts or promises another. We might also call it *rehearsal* time. In our human experience, we often have moments like this: a close brush with death shakes us up and leads us to reinterpret our life in terms of its end. We meet the end in the middle! Similarly, Jesus' prediction about the end of the temple was also a prediction about the end of the world. The end of *a* world was a foretaste of the end of *the* world. In the same way, the outbreak of war, earthquakes, floods, droughts, nuclear or biological catastrophes—each is in some way a rehearsal for the "end of the world." On the one hand, we should not think that the world is actually going to end immediately when these events occur. Jesus warned us that "all these things must happen, but the end is not yet" (see Matthew 24:6). On the other hand, however, they are signs, warnings of:

1. the fragility of human existence;
2. the importance of coming to terms with ultimate values in life;
3. the divine judgment that will be final and inevitable.

Thus each shaking of our security is a call for conversion.

If we ask then, where do we today stand in this timetable laid out by Revelation, one could say that we are in the millennium inaugurated by the blood of Jesus and the martyrs. At times we may think the outbreak of evil is so great that we are now on the eve of the final battle. But if we remember that the timeline is also a spiral, then the outbreak of evil might not be a sign of the end—but elements of the great tribulation we are seeing replayed in our time (as John saw Nero replayed in Domitian). It is not unlike the Einsteinian space-time warp where what seems like a straight line is really a curve: we are *back* to the future! But these replays of tribulation, like the first great tribulation, will serve to move the church forward toward a deeper experience of the millennium. All of this will be in preparation for the new heaven and the new earth where every promise is fulfilled.

Apocalypse Now: Its Meaning for Us Today. If you have followed this commentary with your personal reflection, prayer, and possibly sharing with others, no doubt you have already come to appreciate the Book of Revelation as an inspired message addressed to you. These concluding comments are intended to supplement your emerging personal synthesis and the practical applications already suggested at various points in this commentary.

While John is certainly concerned about the future that lay before his churches, it is evident that this book was not written to satisfy the curiosity of the reader—ancient or modern—about that future in detail. He was convinced the church was on the brink of terrible suffering. But he draws his images of the future from well-known Jewish tradition. It is less important for him to identify specific events and characters than it is to use this drama as a revelatory dream to awaken the present generation to the seriousness of their Christian commitment.

So if today we have reason to feel on the brink of cosmic disaster, it would be well to learn from John some discipline for our curiosity about the future. We do, on the other hand, have some reason to believe that we are living in the millennium during which the activity of Satan is restrained by the gospel sown in blood of Christ and his martyrs. This was John's view of the more distant future to follow the great tribulation. About the millennium he gives us no details other than its relative peace, and the reign of Christ and the martyrs. What is essential is that we live our Christian commitment now, so we share in that reign.

In either case, what is important to know in the end is not what the future holds but *who holds the future*. The end, the "last" *(eschatos)*, is not an event but a person, Jesus Christ. By holding fast to him, we already possess the end and the victory.

In this context, the rich imagery of Revelation nourishes our faith and our personal and liturgical prayer. Symbols, whether numbers, colors, animals, rivers, or trees, speak powerfully to the spirit. They go beyond rational analysis and tug at the heart. They draw us into mystery, before which we (like the heavenly assembly) can only fall down in worship. History is as much in the hand of God as creation itself. But we are not merely invited by the text to gaze upon the glories of heaven. Our attention is also directed to what is happening on earth.

More importantly, it is the relationship between the heavenly and earthly activity that challenges us. For the Christian, faith is not "pie in the sky" living. Nor is it a surrender to the wholly secular forces of a world that thinks it can get along without God. The kingdom of God (which the Christian prays will come as he or she prays the Lord's Prayer), is indeed from heaven, but it comes on earth. The church's earthly activity *now* collaborates toward the coming of that kingdom.

This first appears in John's letters to the churches. These are epistolary visitations by an imprisoned prophet. They are warnings aimed at preparing the churches not for the final judgment but for the historical judgment about to fall upon them in the "great tribulation." John first of all affirms the strengths of each church (with one exception). In doing so he alerts us to look first of all at our own giftedness and the giftedness of each of our Christian communities today. This is not for the sake of fostering complacency but to praise and thank God that his grace in us has not been fruitless. Affirmation is as important as challenge. But challenges there are, too, for the churches are beset with weaknesses. Ephesus has lost its first love. Pergamum has countenanced false teaching. Thyatira has compromised with the idolatrous feasts of Rome. Sardis is "dead." Laodicea's love of wealth has lulled it into tepidity.

Our households, our parishes, and our communities may have the same weaknesses. They probably have others. Happy the prophetic voice that can affirm the good, identify the weaknesses, and challenge the negligent and complacent to conversion!

Another way in which the church on earth affects the coming of the kingdom is intercession. The prayers of the saints ascend to the throne of God, then return to the earth to speed up the just, saving plan of God (see commentary on 8:1-6). Nowhere are the suffering Christians told to avenge themselves upon their persecutors. Instead they turn to God, as Jesus did in his torment, trusting that the cross will be turned into a sign of victory.

Finally, though, we must ask ourselves how a book, written to encourage an oppressed people—most of it written to assure martyrs of the value of their sacrifice—can speak to us today, in cultures where the church enjoys a freedom unheard of for the first-century church. Several comments are in order here. First, the church today has, in some areas of the world, suffered and is suffering in ways very similar to the "great tribulation." The blood of Christian martyrs still flows today. What does that say to us and to our world today? Some would doubtless say, "What a waste! Are not there human values more important than attachment to one's religious faith? What is the value of resisting the oppressor unto death merely because the oppressor will not respect my religious beliefs?"

What the martyr is saying, in an absolute and definitive way, is that everyone in the world, including the oppressor, needs to know Jesus Christ. Pope John Paul II made this point in his 1990 encyclical *Redemptoris Missio* (No. 11): "Christian martyrs of all times—including our own—have given and continue to give their lives in order to bear witness… that every human being needs Jesus Christ, who has conquered sin and death, and reconciled mankind to God."

Short of execution, there are still places in the world where it is a crime to be a Christian by openly sharing one's faith or evangelizing others. I lived in such a country for six years. I knew Christians who were beaten and jailed. Reading the Book of Revelation there was like reading the script for the church's life. In other places simply witnessing to Christian values has invited an assassin's bullet. Revelation assures such witnesses that their blood has not been shed in vain.

Second, there is a sense in which we are living in the millennium prophesied by John. After Constantine firmly established himself as emperor and acknowledged his conversion to Christianity (A.D. 306-337), the menace of persecution was no longer on the horizon. In fact, Christianity became the official religion of the empire, though there were sporadic exceptions. Since then, the church has fared better or worse. At least it has not been under the boot of a vast empire. In many parts of the world the church has enjoyed freedom. Satan's activity has been restrained at least to that extent, as the church has grown and prospered throughout the world.

In this more relaxed and favorable atmosphere, it became fashionable to be a Christian. Discipleship had its rewards. To be a Christian no longer meant to risk an early death. With the new scenario began what we might call "cultural

Christianity." One could argue whether in countries of the West (particularly our United States) we are still in this "cultural Christianity"—think of our public religious holidays. Or while still enjoying the freedom of the secular state, are we actually in a post-Christian culture? There is probably a mixture of both.

In any case, there is a difference between our situation and the situation of the churches for which John was writing. They were powerless against the Roman oppressor. There was no way they could humanly change the situation. All they could do was to pray that God would change it and, should they be brought to the ultimate test of martyrdom, give them the grace to be faithful unto death. John was there to assure them that their ultimate sacrifice was worthwhile. It would not only gain them eternal life, it would eventually bring about the kingdom of God on earth.

We, on the other hand, are faced with a different kind of crisis. True, sometimes the forces of the world seem beyond our control. We feel the same powerlessness which our early brothers and sisters felt under the sword of Rome. International wars, terrorism, the drug scene, escalating crime, the breakdown of family life—these and countless other "forces" may make us feel that the Beast is rampant and winning. But it could be the specific demonic seduction of our age to convince us that no power is available.

For the Christian that can never be true: the Lamb has won the war and we, his followers, are merely engaged in clean-up operations. Moreover—and here is where our situation differs from the last-ditch witness of the martyrs—we have, in many of the democratic countries of the world, some opportunities to change things, to improve the world around us, to remove oppressive yokes and unjust structures from our society, to witness and to organize. What would the martyrs of Revelation tell us to do?

Surely they would say, *"Carpe diem!* Use the freedom you have, the opportunities you have, to bring the kingdom from heaven to earth. Make 'Thy Kingdom come' a reality in the world in which you live. The only way we could do it was through the shedding of our blood. If it was that important to us, can it be less important to you?"

The problem is that it very well might. In the midst of a prosperity not unlike that of Laodicea, it is possible to lose sight of the eschatological urgency of the Christian message—to cease to "watch," to stay alert and make the world worthy of the Lamb and God and his children. We might very easily let things slide until, indeed, the surrounding culture becomes once again the Beast before whom the only weapon left is our blood.

The ultimate message of Revelation for today, then, would seem to lie in the meaning of *martus*, which in one form or another appears eighteen times in this book. It came to mean "martyr" only later. In Revelation it means *witness*. While there it means those who witnessed unto their death, the word remains open to that broader New Testament meaning of those who witness to Christ by their lives. Prior to the outbreak of persecution, it meant those who shared their faith not only by preaching and evangelization through the gifts of the Spirit, but also by the holiness of their lives. It did not mean physical retreat from the world, like the sectarians of Qumran who wrote off the possibility of finding God outside their walls. It meant living the gospel *in* the world, transforming family, economic and political life, and the environment.

In some ways it was more difficult than martyrdom, for it meant daily living "in the midst of a crooked and perverse generation" (Phil 2:15) with a constantly renewed commitment: "Let us not grow tired of doing good" (Gal 6:9). The enemy is not the Roman sword but the siren of seduction (a theme that is also sounded in Revelation). Such is the situation many of us find ourselves in today.

Physical martyrdom may not be our call, but in the daily struggle to be faithful witnesses, we follow a "cloud of witnesses" (Heb 12:1) who have paved the way in their blood. By their ultimate sacrifice, they challenge us to be worthy of

Jesus' promise, "Remain faithful unto death, and I will give you the crown of life" (2:10). Indeed, so it was with many of the faithful of John's day who were not called to the ranks of the martyrs, but through daily faithfulness would share their glorious reign (11:18). The fruit of the martyrs' sacrifice was the conversion of much of the world and in the relative peace and opportunity we now enjoy. They promise us that we too will one day know that our lives of witness have brought about the day when "the kingdom of this world now belongs to our Lord and to his Anointed, and he will reign forever and ever" (11:15).

And so we come to the end of the Apocalypse. From its beginning, this book was presented in the form of a letter. Though the bulk of the book seemed to depart from this form and presented us with an apocalyptic drama instead, the closing paragraphs return to the letter form. Today we close our letters with our signature. Since the real writer of the letter is Jesus, it is Jesus who "signs" the letter. It is his message to Christians facing a crisis at the end of the first century.

But it is also a message to us as we come to the end of the twentieth. Working on us with powerful images, leading us through both ecstatic and terrifying sequences, as if in a profound revelatory dream, it now awakens us to the real world in which we live. It invites us now to face that world with new vision and energy—the very vision and energy of Jesus, the Lamb of God, who died and rose that he might bring the Father's kingdom to earth, and who calls us to share in that divine project today.

✧ ✧ ✧

Reflection

The Book of Revelation invites us to look at both Jesus and the world with new eyes. Having listened to the letters to the churches and the visions of John, we see the world as the theater of God's coming kingdom. We are active even now in this unfolding drama through intercession and the witness of daily living. We also see Jesus as the Lamb of God, Lord of Lords, King of Kings, Alpha and Omega, and the bright Morning Star. He is the point of it all. All of these titles of the Lord Jesus and the others used throughout Revelation fire our hope to hasten the completion of history. With the saints and angels, we are inspired to cry out, "Maranatha! Come, Lord Jesus!"

Questions

1. What does the term "Alpha and Omega" mean to us?

Jesus   p. 237-238

p. 240

2. What meaning does the word "come" have for us in our liturgical life? in our prayer life? in our final calling?

p. 238

241

3. Where are we in the timetable laid out in Revelation?

4. What is meant by proleptic or rehearsal time? Have you ever experienced the meaning of your life in this way? Does this help us in interpreting Revelation?

5. After studying Revelation, how are we to live today? What would the martyrs in Revelation say to our generation?

p 250

6. What changes do I want to make, with God's help, in preparation for the end time?

p. 249

7. How does this study of the Book of Revelation change my perspective on life?

Prayer

Jesus, you are the Alpha and the Omega, the Beginning and the End. When I experience storms in my family, my church, and my world, may I keep my eyes fixed on you, as Peter should have done when faced by the wind and the waves. Keep me from demanding a road map when you have said, "I am the way." Keep me from demanding to know in detail what tomorrow holds, when I know it is you who hold all my tomorrows. Amen.

For Further Study

Barclay, W., *Letters to the Seven Churches: A Study of the Second and Third Chapters of the Book of Revelation* (London: SCM, 1964).

Beasley-Murray, G.R., *The Book of Revelation*. New Century Bible (Grand Rapids, Mich.: Eerdmans, 1974).

___ *Jesus and the Future* (London: Macmillan, 1954).

Bloom, H., ed., *The Revelation of St. John the Divine* (New York: Chelsea House, 1988).

Boring, M.E., *Revelation* (Louisville: John Knox, 1989).

Bowman, J.W., *The Revelation to John: Its Dramatic Structure and Message* (Philadelphia: Westminster, 1955).

Caird, G.B., *A Commentary on the Revelation of St. John the Divine. Harper's NT Commentaries* (New York: Harper & Row, 1966). Very good for theological and homiletical insights.

Charles, R.H., *A Critical and Exegetical Commentary on the Revelation of St. John*. 2 vols. The International Critical Commentary (New York: Charles Scribner's Sons, 1920). Classical, lengthy, highly technical, detailed study of John's use of the Old Testament. Though dated in some aspects, still very useful.

Collins, Adela Y., *The Apocalypse. New Testament Message* (series) (Wilmington: Glazier, 1979).

___ "The Apocalypse" in *New Jerome Biblical Commentary* (Englewood Cliffs, Prentice-Hall, 1990), 996-1016.

___ *The Combat Myth in the Book of Revelation* (Missoula, Mont.: Scholars, 1976). Described by the author as "a study of the mythic traditions, the 'old stories' used by John, the new meaning his visions gave to them, and how they fit together to create a new work, the Apocalypse."

___ *Crisis and Catharsis: The Power of the Apocalypse* (Philadelphia: Westminster, 1984). Interesting study of the sociological background of Revelation.

Corsini, E., *The Apocalypse: The Perennial Revelation of Jesus Christ*. F. J. Moloncy, trans. (Wilmington: Michael Glazier, 1983). Views Revelation not as prophetic history of the church from its beginning to the end of time and therefore, future coming of Christ but a meditation on meaning of Christ already come. Beast of Chapter 13 and prostitute of Chapter 17 are not Rome but Judaism—a singular interpretation.

D'Aragon, G.B., *"The Apocalypse,"* in *Jerome Biblical Commentary* (Englewood Cliffs: Prentice-Hall, 1968), Vol. 2, 467-493.

Eller, V., *The Most Revealing Book of the Bible: Making Sense out of Revelation* (Grand Rapids, Mich.: Eerdmans, 1974). Interesting map of salvation history according to Apocalypse.

Ellul, J., *Apocalypse: The Book of Revelation* (New York: Seabury, 1977). Interesting exploration of symbols.

Ewing, Ward. *The Power of the Lamb: Revelation's Theology of Liberation for You* (Cambridge, MA: Cowley, 1990). A stimulating and challenging application of Revelation to North American culture and the Christian struggle against the powers and unjust structures of a post-Christian culture.

Farrer, A.M., *The Revelation of St. John the Divine* (Oxford: Clarendon, 1964). Good for the liturgical background of Revelation.

—-*A Rebirth of Images: The Making of St. John's Apocalypse* (Albany: State University of New York Press, 1989).

Feuillet, A., *The Apocalypse* (Staten Island: Alba House, 1964). Review of earlier literature good.

Fiorenza, E.S., *Invitation to the Book of Revelation* (Garden City, NY: Doubleday Image, 1981).

—-*The Book of Revelation: Justice and Judgment* (Philadelphia: Fortress, 1985). Not a commentary but a fine study of major aspects of Revelation.

Ford, J.M., *Revelation*. Anchor Bible 38 (Garden City: Doubleday, 1975). See the critical review of this work by A.Y. Collins in *CBQ* 38 (1976), 555-57.

Giblin, C.H., *The Book of Revelation: The Open Book of Prophecy* (Collegeville, Minn.: Michael Glazier, 1991).

Glasson, T.F., *The Revelation of John* (Cambridge: Cambridge University Press, 1965).

Harrington, W., *Understanding the Apocalypse* (Washington DC: Corpus, 1969). Lengthy introduction treating major questions and the theology of Revelation.

Hughes, P.E., *The Book of Revelation: A Commentary* (Grand Rapids, Mich.: Eerdmans).

Kealy, S.p., *The Apocalypse of John* (Collegeville, Minn.: Michael Glazier, 1987).

Kiddle, M., *The Revelation of St. John* (London: Hodder & Stoughton, 1963).

Laws, S., *In the Light of the Lamb: Imagery, Parody and Theology in the Apocalypse of John* (Wilmington: Glazier, 1988).

LeFrois, B.J., *The Woman Clothed with the Sun: Apoc. 12* (Rome: Herder & Herder, 1953).

Minear, P.S., *I Saw a New Earth* (Washington: Corpus, 1968). Serious attempt to get beyond limited application to first century and find relevance for today. But see the important introduction by M.M. Bourke.

Mounce, R.H., *The Book of Revelation* (Grand Rapids, Mich.: Eerdmans, 1977).

Perkins, P., *Revelation;* in *Collegeville Bible Commentary* (Collegeville, Minn.: Liturgical Press, 1988) 1265-1300.

Peterson, E.H., *Reversed Thunder: The Revelation of John and the Praying Imagination* (San Francisco: Harper & Row, 1988).

Randall, John, *The Book of Revelation—What Does It Really Say?* (Locust Valley, N.Y.: Living Flame, 1976). Popular but well-founded. Good as response to literalist application to our times.

Rowland, Christopher, *The Open Heaven: A Study of Apocalyptic in Judaism and Early Christianity* (New York: Crossroads, 1982). Bibliography given.

Shepherd, M.H., Jr., *The Paschal Liturgy and the Apocalypse* Ecumenical Studies I, Worship 6 (Richmond: John Knox, 1960).

Stringfellow, W., *An Ethic for Christians and Other Aliens in a Strange Land* (Waco, TX: Word Books, 1973). An application of Revelation to contemporary American life.

Sweet, J.P.M., *Revelation* (Philadelphia: Westminster, 1979). Interesting chart.

Swete, H.B., *The Apocalypse of St. John* (Grand Rapids, Mich.: Eerdmans, 1909) (London: Macmillan, 1909).

Torrey, C.C., *The Apocalypse of John* (Yale University Press, 1958).

Vos, L.A., *The Synoptic Traditions in the Apocalypse* (Amsterdam: Kampen, 1965).